EXPLORATORY RESEARCH IN THE SOCIAL SCIENCES

ROBERT A. STEBBINS

Qualitative Research Methods
Volume 48

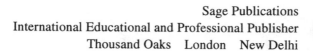

Sage Publications
International Educational and Professional Publisher
Thousand Oaks   London   New Delhi

For information:

Sage Publications, Inc.
2455 Teller Road
Thousand Oaks, California 91320
E-mail: order@sagepub.com

Sage Publications Ltd.
6 Bonhill Street
London EC2A 4PU
United Kingdom

Sage Publications India Pvt. Ltd.
M-32 Market
Greater Kailash I
New Delhi 110 048 India

Printed in the United States of America

Library of Congress Cataloging-in-Publication Data

Stebbins, Robert A., 1938-
    Exploratory research in the social sciences / by Robert A. Stebbins.
       p.   cm.
    Includes bibliographical references.
    ISBN 0-7619-2398-5 (cloth: alk. paper)
    ISBN 0-7619-2399-3 (pbk.: alk. paper)
    1. Social sciences—Research. 2. Social sciences—Methodology.
I. Title. II. Series.
  H62.S754 2001
  300'.7'2—dc21   00-012753

01   02   03   04   05   10 9 8 7 6 5 4 3 2 1

Acquiring Editor:	Heidi Van Middlesworth
Production Editor:	Denise Santoyo
Editorial Assistant:	Kathryn Journey
Typesetter:	Janelle LeMaster

When citing a university paper, please use the proper form. Remember to cite the Sage University Paper series title and include the paper number. One of the following formats can be adapted (depending on the style manual used):

(1) Stebbins, R. A. (2001) *Exploratory Research in the Social Sciences.* Sage University Papers Series on Qualitative Research Methods, Vol. 48. Thousand Oaks, CA: Sage.

OR

(2) Stebbins, R. A. (2001). *Exploratory Research in the Social Sciences.* (Sage University Papers Series on Qualitative Research Methods, Vol. 48). Thousand Oaks, CA: Sage.

CONTENTS

SERIES EDITOR'S INTRODUCTION

Research in any field begins with curiosity. Yet method texts often read as primers on how to kill curiosity by subjecting it to formula. As a social process, all research involves a good deal of guesswork, fumbling about, looking around, following rather loosely formulated hunches, filling in empty spaces and, generally, figuring out ways to usefully categorize and explain what it is that one has learned. Exploration is in many ways simply a synonym for research of even the most systematic sort since stumbling over something previously unseen or unknown is presumably the sort of experience that all students seek. Exploration, with its open character and emphasis on flexibility, pragmatism, and the particular, biographically specific interests of an investigator, is arguably a more inviting and indeed accurate way of representing social research than treating it as a narrowing, quasi rule-bound and discipline-based process that settles and confirms rather than unsettles and questions what one knows.

This is—in rough form—the premise that Robert Stebbins elaborates in *Exploratory Research in the Social Sciences,* the 48th volume in the Sage Series on Qualitative Methods. Exploratory work has long been characterized as a brief, fleeting, preliminary stage in the research process that gives way—the sooner the better—to the real thing. As this work suggests however taking exploration to be merely a rehearsal for the main show leads to an unnecessarily stiff and stifling view of social study. Exploration is perhaps better thought of as a perspective, a way of approaching and carrying out a social study (including, importantly, reporting on what has been learned). Further, as a way to talk about methods, exploration is attractive and helps move current methodological discussions beyond listing the pros and cons associated with a set of tired, oversimplified, either-or choices —qualitative or quantitative, inductive or deductive, descriptive or predictive. As put forward here, social research is always (or at least should be) exploratory: a long, cumulative, choice-laden, and interest-governed process in which no single study can be definitive.

Such an open perspective on social research is welcome in these methodologically charged and changing times. Exploratory research is about putting one's self deliberately in a place—again and again—where discovery is possible and broad, usually (but not always) nonspecialized interests can be pursued. This is the sort of research outlined and exemplified by C. Wright Mills as intellectual craftsmanship and results in the sort of theory celebrated by Anslem Strauss and Barney Glaser as grounded. While labor intensive to be sure, exploratory research requires lengthy periods of fieldwork (of various kinds) and the sort of personal concern and long standing interest in a topical area that sustains such fieldwork. From topic, however, to concept because, as Professor Stebbins argues, building useful theory is the reason d'être of research. Clarification and understanding are joined only by concepts that move past the singular and individual. How such concepts emerge is at the center of this slim volume and, in the end, definitional of solid exploratory research.

John Van Maanen
Peter K. Manning
Marc L. Miller

INTRODUCTION

Strange as it may seem, *exploration* is turning out to be one of the world's more enigmatic ideas. Well beyond the research world of the social scientist, which is the scope of this book, I get the impression that, generally, people raised today on this planet view exploration as an outmoded process. Taking the North American attitude as an example, exploration is regarded as something Columbus was enamored of, which then got into the blood of the French voyageurs and American mountain men, and shortly thereafter was forgotten—a mere prologue to the main drama of developing American and Canadian societies with the aid of science and technology. Serious people, if modern common sense is any authority, need not explore, for they now have established rules, theories, and procedures with which to solve their problems, be those problems scientific, administrative, communal, or domestic. Exploration, if it is given any thought at all, is typically seen as messy, without direction, time consuming, and fraught with possible disappointment, among many other unwanted qualities. Who needs exploration when established procedures presumably exist to help solve life's myriad problems?

But is this widespread faith in *formulas*—my shorthand term for established rules, theories, and procedures—really warranted? No. First, people everywhere scarcely know all they could usefully know about the physical and social world in which they live. For instance, many cancers and other life-threatening diseases still have no cures, and confusion reigns about the true nature of contemporary global weather patterns and the fluctuations in national economies that so successfully defy prediction these days. In these areas, formulas are either nonexistent or, if they exist, inadequate for the job. Second, individuals in every society are always learning something new about their everyday lives. Using essentially exploratory (and sometimes serendipitous) procedures, people discover through their own experience and powers of reasoning the most efficient route to the office, now that the old route is closed for repairs; the cause of a colleague's tendency toward tempermental outbursts; or the annoying limitations of a new household tool or appliance. Third, a number of amateur-professional fields rely· heavily on exploratory procedures, most of which are found in the sciences and the fine and popular arts. Fourth, Columbus-style or in outer space, exploration is still going on, in fact, although now mostly under water and in space beyond the earth's atmosphere. Sometimes, exploration in these different areas is needed because the world has changed and the old formulas no longer fit sufficiently well (e.g., the routes to the office). At other times, the phenomenon under consideration is still poorly understood, as in the cure for certain cancers and the nature of life on other planets.

My aim in this book is to argue for the present and continuing significance of exploration in the social sciences, a goal that is accomplished in six chapters. I start by examining the nature and importance of this idea. I turn next to the ways social scientists explore, then to some of the problems they encounter when writing exploratory research, and then to the way of life they are forced to adopt as social scientific explorers. The final chapter centers on the future of exploration in society and the social sciences. Midway through the text, I present several examples of exploratory research. In this exposition, I have been guided by the following precept: To understand well any phenomenon, it is necessary to start by looking at it in broad, nonspecialized terms. In other words, first observe the woods, then study its individual trees. The modern tendency to rely on formulas inverts this precept, causing no small number of people to get lost in the forest while also contributing to the intractable problems of incomplete explanation of and faulty prediction about social life.

In keeping with the precept of the big picture, this book is intended to be general; it is more than a primer or manual on how to conduct exploratory research in the social sciences, a subject also covered by, among others, Glaser and Strauss (1967), Glaser (1978), and Lofland and Lofland (1995). I do, of course, expect it to have practical utility for researchers who would take up social science exploration or, having taken it up, would like to learn more about it. In this book, exploration is portrayed as something larger than a special scientific process and methodological approach; I also see it as an all-encompassing personal orientation that tends to dominate the social scientist's everyday consciousness from conception of an exploratory project through research design and data collection to writing of the final report. It is this general outlook—referred to later as a way of life, a lifestyle—that I also want to examine here, along with its consequences for researchers and their research.

On what authority do I write such a book? I write in part from my own experience as an exploratory researcher, which began in 1967 when I started collecting data on the problems petty criminals experience after leaving prison; this was followed by research on teachers' definitions of classroom situations, a string of a dozen studies in the field of serious leisure (the leisure of amateurs, hobbyists, "career" volunteers), and a couple of studies of Canadian francophones living in minority circumstances. And I am still exploring serious leisure, at present the low- and high-risk sports of kayaking, snowboarding, and mountain climbing as pursued in the Canadian Rockies. In addition to the publications resulting from these projects, I have, on occasion, expressly addressed myself to the question of exploration (Shaffir & Stebbins, 1991, pp. 1-24; Stebbins, 1992a, 1997b, 1997c).

Furthermore, I have accumulated considerable experience teaching graduate students about exploration. Over the years, I have conducted numerous graduate seminars and individual tutorials on qualitative methods, with exploration always being a central topic of lectures and discussion. In addition, I have supervised or helped supervise more than 50 master's and doctoral theses reporting exploratory work, not only in sociology and leisure studies, my two disciplines, but also in nursing, social work, education, psychology, anthropology, environmental design, and community health science.

Yet, for myself, I have never received formal training in exploration, although I doubt such training was available during my graduate school days in the early 1960s, had I even been inclined to seek it at that time. Indeed, the term seems to have first entered the sociologist's lexicon in 1967, with publication of Glaser and Strauss's (1967) seminal volume *The Discovery of Grounded Theory*. To be sure, sociologists and anthropologists had explored long before that year (the Chicago School studies in sociology and the ethnographies of the British social anthropologists, for example, date to the early decades of the past century), but they seem rarely, if ever, to have had any interest in discussing in print this process. Still, I did have the good fortune to be exploring criminal lifestyles when Glaser and Strauss's book was released and have lived to the present with its reception in social science circles. That reception in the social sciences, in general, has been very gradual, to be sure, even if many contemporary qualitative researchers, in particular, consider it something of a methodological bible. For me, it is still the greatest single treatise on qualitative social science, even though the words *exploration* and *discovery* appear there only sporadically. In many ways, my work in this book can be understood as a complement to what these authors wrote.

A theory can be proved by experiment;
but no path leads from experiment to the birth of a theory.

Albert Einstein, The Sunday Times, *18 July 1976*

EXPLORATORY RESEARCH IN THE SOCIAL SCIENCES

ROBERT A. STEBBINS
University of Calgary

1. WHAT IS EXPLORATION?

It was observed in the Introduction that adventuresome folk explore in art, space (air, land, water), science, and everyday life. Notwithstanding this vast domain where exploration sometimes or frequently occurs, its recognition as an important procedure and personal orientation is generally missing in the modern world. In the social sciences, including even qualitative research circles, the idea of exploration is usually mentioned, if at all, only in passing, a short statement by Blumer (1969, pp. 40-42) and Glaser and Strauss's (1967) *The Discovery of Grounded Theory* being two main exceptions. And still earlier, Boulding (1958) wrote about the need to "travel over a field of study" with the object of extending "the reader's field of acquaintance with the complex cases of the real world" (p. 5).

Part of the reluctance to broach the subject of exploration, I believe, stems from a poor understanding of what it is. But the chief problem, it seems, is that exploration is simply on neither the common mind nor the scholarly one; for many people, researchers and nonresearchers alike, it is plainly irrelevant. Thus, Blumer's (1969) observation still holds. "Consid-

1

ering the crucial need and value of exploratory research in the case of the social and psychological sciences, it is an odd commentary on these sciences that their current methodological preoccupations are practically mute on this type of research" (p. 42).

It might appear that this picture of neglect is starting to fade, for many contemporary social science textbooks in methodology, in sections running from a paragraph to two or three pages, do treat exploration clearly identified and discussed as such (e.g., Adler & Clark, 1999, p. 9; Palys, 1997, pp. 77-79). Although this is hardy enough in light of Blumer's comment, perhaps its advocates should be thankful for small favors. Nevertheless, notwithstanding such "honorable mention," today's standard textbook treatments of exploration, as near as I can tell, are still bereft of a substantial definition and elaboration of this idea.

Defining Exploration

Poor understanding of the idea is rooted in significant part in the different senses in which the main dictionaries of the English language define the verb *to explore*. One sense is to study, examine, analyze, or investigate something; this is the most general meaning of the four presented here. A second sense, which is far more specific, is to become familiar with something by testing it or experimenting with it. This is exploration as conducted by artists, inventors, and innovators. In still another sense, *explore* means to travel over or through a particular space for the purposes of discovery and adventure, what is referred to in the Introduction as spatial exploration. A final sense is to examine a thing or idea for diagnostic purposes, to search it systematically for something. This meaning suggests that, because the explorer already knows what to look for (e.g., oil, cancer, toxins), he or she need only methodically hunt for it.

Exploration, in the first sense, is little more than a handy synonym for the inquisitive processes of examining, investigating, and the like. This type—*investigative exploration*—describes what social science explorers do, but it does so only in the most general way. The second definition, although closer than the first to the essence of social science exploration, is distinguished by the fact that the testing or experimenting in question is done to create a particular effect or product, as manifested in a new painting, culinary dish, combination of musical sounds, or method or device. In this—*innovative exploration*—the goal is to gain only the degree of familiarity with the properties of substances and procedures that is needed to manipulate them so as to achieve the desired effect or product. The inclination to explore is satiated, once this effect or product has been created. This is the principal difference separating innovative exploration from the third sense, *exploration for discovery*. In the latter, research is not finished until everything of importance for describing and understanding the area under study has been discovered. In other words, exploration for discovery aims to be as broad and thorough as possible, whereas exploration leading to innovation is narrower and more focused. The fourth sense—it can be labeled *limited exploration*—stands out for the explorer's interest in searching systematically for something in particular. Here, because the explorer knows what to look for, innovation and broad discovery, if important at all, are decidedly secondary goals.

It is possible to define social science exploration by combining the concept of exploration for discovery with certain new elements not mentioned in any of the four senses just considered. Indeed, because none exists, it is imperative to create such a definition, even though Vogt (1999, p. 105), to his credit, at least offers a helpful definition of exploratory research. The following definition is, however, more consistent than his with the argument presented in this book:

Social science exploration is a broad-ranging, purposive, systematic, prearranged undertaking designed to maximize the discovery of generalizations leading to description and understanding of an area of social or psychological life. Such exploration is, depending on the standpoint taken, a distinctive way of conducting science—a scientific process—a special methodological approach (as contrasted with confirmation), and a pervasive personal orientation of the explorer. The emergent generalizations are many and varied; they include the descriptive facts, folk concepts, cultural artifacts, structural arrangements, social processes, and beliefs and belief systems normally found there.

It would not be difficult to broaden this definition to include all science. One need only stipulate that the generalizations discovered pertain to an area of social, psychological, or physical life and then follow this up with appropriate examples. And yes, exploration does occur in physical science, for example, astronomy, mineralogy, and entomology, where it is often conducted by amateurs who, in part, are needed because professionals alone cannot systematically cover all of outer space or the surface of the earth (Stebbins, 1978).

Exploration and its cousin, serendipity, constitute two distinct forms of discovery. Serendipity is the quintessential form of informal experimentation, accidental discovery, and spontaneous invention. It contrasts sharply with exploration, just described as a broad-ranging, purposive, systematic, prearranged undertaking. The first is highly democratic—at least in principle, anyone can experience it—whereas the second is more narrowly select, the province of those creative people who must routinely produce new ideas. In certain fields of serious leisure and professional work, artists, scientists, and entertainers, for example, routinely explore, whereas, in some forms of casual leisure, the people at play (both children and adults), the sociable conversationalists, and the seekers of sensory stimulation never do this (Stebbins, 1997a), an observation that holds equally well for many nonprofessional kinds of work. For the second group, new ideas and other discoveries can only come by way of serendipity; for the first group, discovery, although occasionally serendipitous, is nonetheless far more likely to flow from exploration. Robert Merton (1957), possibly the only social scientist to discuss the idea in any detail, described the following instance of sociological serendipity:

> In the course of our research into the social organization of Craftown, a suburban housing community of some 700 families, largely of working class status, we observed that a large proportion of the residents were affiliated with more civic, political, and other voluntary organizations than had been the case in their previous places of residence. Quite incidentally, we noted further that this increase in group participation had occurred also among the parents of infants and young children. This finding was rather inconsistent with commonsense knowledge. For it is well known that, particularly on the lower economic levels, youngsters usually tie parents down and preclude their taking active part in organized group life outside the home. (p. 105)

Merton went on to note that "we were at once confronted, then, by an anomalous fact which was certainly no part of our original program of observation" (p. 106).

That social science researchers qua researchers have more in common with amateur and professional physical scientists than with participants in casual leisure suggests that the first should rely not on accidental serendipity but instead try to discover new ideas by systematically exploring social groups, processes, and activities. To accomplish this, however, they must intentionally put themselves in a position to make discoveries, rather than carrying out their daily research agenda by passively awaiting the moment when they are struck, as it were, with serendipity. Amateur scientists, nearly all of whom conduct exploratory research, know well this distinction (Stebbins, 1978, pp. 240-241). In those areas of social science where discovery should be regularized, researchers would do well to emulate the methodological approach of their counterparts in serious leisure.

Exploration is not a synonym for *qualitative research,* a much broader idea that is subject to many different definitions. In general, the first emphasizes development of theory from data, whereas the second emphasizes methodology and the actual collection of data by which this development is accomplished (see, for example, the definition of qualitative research in Denzin & Lincoln, 1994, p. 2). No doubt many qualitative researchers would complain that this is an unfair depiction of their profession, contending that they do indeed consider theory development a principal aim of their empirical efforts. But when they identify themselves using this label, it tends to obscure this part of their scientific work. The next section shows, moreover, that qualitative elements are found in most kinds of social science research, including many at the confirmatory level. Here, because exploration is not part of confirmatory procedure, using the qualitative descriptor masks even more the role of exploration as a crucial scientific process. Finally, among those qualitative researchers who do know what exploration is and how to go about it are found some who fail to recognize the manifold ramifications of this process. As this book demonstrates throughout, they allow any number of confirmatory practices and procedures to insinuate themselves in their research and writing routines.

The Process of Exploration

Evaluating the contributions of exploratory research projects, especially the first one or two in a new field of inquiry, constitutes one of the areas where social scientists are often found wandering among the trees, having lost sight of the forest. Their tendency is to appraise the initial study in the new field as though it were a confirmatory undertaking; they fret over matters of design—notably, sampling, validity, and generalizability—and over the literature review and, in doing this, tend to minimize the importance of the original ideas that have just been brought to light. Apart from the issue of the literature review, which will be taken up later, this style of evaluation is rooted in a failure to see exploration as a process that unfolds not only within individual studies but also across several studies. (Indeed, the same can be said for confirmation or verification.) The critics are unaware that early weaknesses in sampling, validity, and generalizability tend to get corrected over the course of several exploratory studies, in a process referred to later in this chapter as *concatenation.*

Researchers explore when they have little or no scientific knowledge about the group, process, activity, or situation they want to examine but nevertheless have reason to believe it contains elements worth discovering. To explore effectively a given phenomenon, they must approach it with two special orientations: *flexibility* in looking for data and *open-mindedness* about where to find them. Oriented thus, the first step is to proceed according to Max Weber's model to acquire an intimate, firsthand understanding (*Verstehen*) of the human acts being observed. It follows that the most efficacious approach is to search for this understanding wherever it may be found, using any ethical method that would appear to bear fruit. The outcome of these procedures and the main goal of exploratory research is the production of inductively derived generalizations about the group, process, activity, or situation under study. Next, the researcher weaves these generalizations into a *grounded theory* explaining the object of study, the construction of which, I find, is most clearly described in a set of publications by Glaser and Strauss (1967) and Glaser (1978, 1995, pp. 3-17).

The left side of Figure 1 shows that both quantitative and qualitative data may be gathered during exploration. In other words, although in most exploratory studies, qualitative data predominate, they are augmented where possible and desirable with such descriptive statistics as indexes, percentages, and frequency distributions. Indeed, some researchers even conduct quantitative surveys as a subsequent part of their investigation, asking respondents fixed-response questions predicated on the qualitative data gathered previously. As a scientist or group of scientists come to understand more clearly the group or activity chosen for examination, they and their field of research move to the right across Figure 1. As they proceed in this direction, they come to rely less and less on exploration and more and more on prediction and confirmation, as carried out along the lines of one or more hypotheses derived deductively from the grounded theory that has been emerging since the first study. This process typically unfolds over the course of several studies, each executed in concatenated fashion with reference to the earlier ones (Stebbins, 1992b). In other words, movement across Figure 1 is paralleled by an expansion of the grounded theory and the development of generic or overarching concepts (Prus, 1987), both made possible by the accumulation of research and application of the theory to an ever wider range of phenomena.

The far right side of Figure 1 represents the final stages of the scientific process, as seen in a coherent grounded theory about a reasonably broad range of related phenomena. At this point, concern is chiefly with enhanc-

7

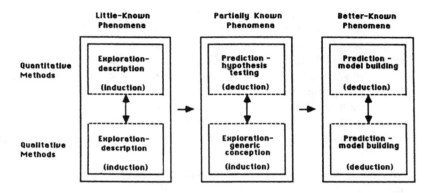

Figure 1. The relationship of qualitative and quantitative methods.
SOURCE: Shaffir and Stebbins, 1991. Reprinted with permission of Sage Publications.

ing precision of the theory, a process commonly pursued through prediction, quantification, and a heavy reliance on inferential statistics. Even here, however, qualitative data occasionally play an important role. Such data, for example, can help confirm propositions not amenable to quantitative assessment or, through exploration, bring to light important recent changes in social process and social structure that the narrower focus of hypothesis confirmation has led researchers to overlook.

Before moving on, a couple of general comments about Figure 1 are in order. First, in terms of amount of time devoted to and amount of research carried out in each cell, it is not drawn to scale. For instance, it is likely that more research is carried on in the second two cells than in the first one. In addition, it is more accurate to qualify exploration as *primarily* inductive and confirmation as *primarily* deductive. In other words, during an exploratory study, researchers do think deductively at times, although they do so largely within their emerging theoretical framework rather than within established theory and a set of hypotheses deduced from it. Moreover, they engage in confirmation, but what they confirm are their emergent generalizations rather than an ensemble of a priori predictions. Confirmatory researchers, for their part, despite constraints of research design, sometimes serendipitously observe regularities leading to generalizations about the group, process, activity, or situation they are investigating. Some of these chance discoveries may have been reached by inductive reasoning, but, in confirmatory work, such induction is not systematic. Thus, it is advisable that social science researchers who want to be unequivocally clear about the nature and scope of their research describe it as qualitative-exploratory, quantitative-exploratory, qualitative-confirmatory, or quantitative-confirmatory. Not surprisingly, the simpler labels of qualitative and quantitative can engender confusion.

Exploration and inductive reasoning are important in science in part because deductive logic alone can never uncover new ideas and observations. As Urdang Associates (1985) puts it,

> With the growth of natural science philosophers became increasingly aware that a deductive argument ... can only bring out what is already implicit in its premises, and hence inclined to insist that all new knowledge must come from some form of induction. (p. 159)

The limits of deductive argument are effectively illustrated in what I will refer to from time to time as *syllogistic reasoning*. The syllogism is the simplest of all deductive systems, where all A is B, all B is C, and therefore all A is C. In this system, it is impossible through logic alone to learn about propositions D, E, and F, because the reasoning connecting propositions A, B, and C amounts to a closed argument. Given that established social science theory is a vast, albeit less logically tight version of the simple syllogism, it, too, is incapable of revealing any information about the social equivalents of D, E, and F. Whether D, E, F, and still other propositions even exist and, if they exist, whether any of them are important for a detailed and profound understanding of the group, process, activity, or situation in question can only be determined through discovery. In principle, social scientists have a choice at this point: explore—that is, use inductive logic—or wait for serendipity to light the way. But serendipity, as already argued, is too adventitious and sporadic to serve as a substitute for systematic exploration.

The preceding two paragraphs help explain why computerized programs for qualitative research, several versions of which are now on the market, can do no more than ease the burden of routine analytic tasks, among them, coding data, typing up fieldnotes, and sorting and comparing codes. As Dohan and Sánchez-Jankowski (1998) note,

> Computer assistance cannot make up for the shortcomings in the researcher's basic talent to interpret. ... The [real] work of [qualitative data analysis] lies in the annotation and rewriting of notes, in the conceptualization and develop-

ment of a coding scheme, and in the art of proposing reasonable hypotheses. (p. 494)

In other words, the computer is, no more or no less, a fantastic deductive instrument.

In general, exploration is the preferred methodological approach under at least three conditions: when a group, process, activity, or situation has received little or no systematic empirical scrutiny, has been largely examined using prediction and control rather than flexibility and open-mindedness, or has grown to maturity along the continuum described in Figure 1 but has changed so much along the way that it begs to be explored anew. Whichever condition pertains, the accent in exploration is forever on the inductive generation of new concepts and empirical generalizations.

Figure 1 raises the thorny question of when in the sequence of studies to make the transition from exploration to confirmation. In particular, newcomers to discovery research often wonder when exploration has gone far enough, when it has reached its point of diminishing returns. They also ask how broad must a research problem be before it qualifies for exploratory treatment?

Exploration and Confirmation

Scientific exploration and confirmation—the two main methodological approaches in the social sciences—are probably more similar than different, even though their main goals diverge sharply. Consider, first, some of the differences. In terms of goals, exploration aims to generate new ideas and weave them together to form grounded theory, or theory that emerges directly from data (Glaser & Strauss, 1967). These ideas are the raison d'être of the enterprise, and everything else—study design, measurement techniques, received theory without an exploratory base—is subordinate to them. By contrast, in confirmatory research, the research design (including sampling and statistical treatment of data) reigns supreme. The goal here is to test hypotheses, and the goodness of the test hinges on the quality of the design. Indeed, the art of confirmatory research is most evident in the imaginativeness with which the study is conceived. As Kirk and Miller (1986) put it, "Most of the technology of 'confirmatory' nonqualitative research in both the social and natural sciences is aimed at preventing discovery" (p. 15). At the other end of the spectrum, the art of exploratory research is evident in the ideas that emerge from data. A second set of crucial differences is found in research procedure. It was mentioned earlier that exploration requires flexibility and open-mindedness, differing from confirmation and its reliance on *control* of variables and *prediction* of outcomes using hypotheses.

Thus, exploration comes to a halt temporarily in a particular area, when researchers there believe that no significant new ideas can come from further open-ended investigation and pressing confirmatory issues begin to dominate. Yet even though a program of exploration can bring a field to the point of diminishing returns in new ideas, it is still better to abide by the rule, when in doubt explore, rather than by its opposite, when in doubt confirm. Following the first rule avoids premature theoretical closure and the failure to discover something of importance, a far more deleterious situation than failing to start confirming key ideas, a process researchers can always initiate at a later date. Moreover, because social life changes, more rapidly today than ever (see Chapter 6), a program of continuous exploration is good practice even in well-explored fields, to ensure that new developments will find their way into established theory and to avoid the narrowness that comes of syllogistic reasoning.

And how many *well-explored* fields are there in social science? Very few. Entire disciplines still seem to have little to do with this approach, most notably economics and political science. Although the different branches of sociology vary as to the extent of their exploratory base, none that I know of started out free of a heavy dose of a priori armchair theorizing. Sociology has always been a theory-driven discipline, and historically, that theory has not been of the grounded variety.

Yet exploration and confirmation do resemble each other in a fundamental way. The portraits of qualitative and quantitative exploration sketched in this book suggest that they are most accurately viewed as solid members of the positivist tradition in the social sciences. This alleged cozy relationship between these two approaches may alarm those qualitative researchers who look warily on positivists as the methodological enemy, as malevolent people driven in good measure by the hope of effecting a scientific cleansing. John Lofland (1995), who is certainly aware of the affinity of "analytic ethnography" (roughly equivalent to the idea of exploration being developed here) with interpretive social science, explains why he nevertheless places this kind of ethnography squarely in the positivist camp:

> Most fundamentally, work of an analytically ethnographic bent has been and remains to this day one variety of mainstream or even positivistic strategies of social research, sharing much with the strategies of experiments, surveys, and historical comparisons. Among these shared features is the framing of one's

task as the asking of basic questions about the domain of human social life and organization combined with striving to formulate empirically falsifiable and generically attuned answers to those questions.

The main questions asked in analytically ethnographically inclined research have been—and are—very much the same as the questions asked by most other social researchers and by people in every viable society about almost everything. (p. 37)

These questions center on types, causes, frequencies, and magnitudes as well as on structures, processes, and consequences. Some of them are related to agency, or how people strategize in or toward the phenomenon being studied.

I have raised the question of positivism and the stance Lofland takes on its kinship with analytic ethnography to reassure social science researchers that, in promoting exploration as a navigable passage to the land of a theoretically rejuvenated social science, I am not also asking them to abandon their positivist ways to sail there. I am convinced, as Lofland obviously is, that the similarities between exploration and confirmation far outnumber their differences, the latter being found chiefly in the antinomies of induction/deduction, flexibility/control, and prediction/open-mindedness. Furthermore, as part of positivist social science, exploration is not an obscure, mysterious process available only to a small coterie of insightful intellectual adventurers. On the contrary, anyone with the will to explore can do it, and I am convinced that social science theory would profit enormously were more of its researchers inclined to work in the field of discovery.

Social science exploration is positivistic, in part, because it is nomothetic, its principle goal being production of valid generalizations about a type of group, process, activity, or situation. As such, it falls outside the world of idiographic research, which is a main enterprise in the humanities, defined here as the study of religion, philosophy, ancient history, languages, and literature. Examinations of particular historical events, literary figures, written works, and the like, where no generalization beyond the object of research is intended, fall in a different tradition of knowledge. Now, I am in no way belittling this tradition, for its scholarly devotees have revealed a great deal of considerable significance about important events, people, and cultural objects. No matter that there was no war like World War II, no man like Julius Caesar, no book like *Crime and Punishment*; in themselves, they were, and still are, important and influential.

One reason for their importance is that scientific exploration, in its quest for generalizations, overlooks the unique features of its objects of study to provide only a cross-sectional view of, say, all world wars, world leaders, or Russian novels. It is also true, however, that much of the time, exploration centers on groups, processes, activities, or situations whose individual uniquenesses are not important or influential in any broad sense and so nothing of scientific value is lost when they are ignored. When I explored the world of the men who play Canadian football (Stebbins, 1993a), all of the amateurs and most of the professionals I met could have been considered ordinary players with no significant influence on either the present or the future of their sport or the society in which they lived. Nevertheless, it was fruitful to explore this world for generalizations about Canadian football as a serious leisure activity and form of professional work.

Finally, I do not wish to go on record as saying that humanist scholars do not occasionally explore in their research. Quite the contrary. The principal difference is that, when they examine singular events or cultural items, they avoid making broad generalizations about them as types. Nevertheless, they might, for instance, systematically explore a set of documents in search of whatever additional causes of World War II they might reveal or read all texts written by or about Julius Caesar in an attempt to discover more about his personality. Science tries to give laws covering many cases; one main interest in the humanities lies chiefly in saying something significant about particular cases.

Concatenation

The expression *concatenated exploration* refers at once to a research process and the resulting set of field studies that are linked together, as it were, in a chain leading, to cumulative grounded or inductively generated theory. Studies near the beginning of the chain are wholly or predominantly exploratory in scope. Each study or link in the chain examines or, at times, reexamines a related group, activity, or social process or aspect of a broader category of groups or social processes. Exploration describes the nature of the overall approach to data collection that is followed, especially at the beginning of the chain or concatenation, but to a significant degree all along it as well. Exploration may be qualitative or quantitative (Glaser & Strauss, 1967, Chapter 8), although most researchers in this area seem to favor mixing the two, with the first being primary and the second being secondary. Still, as the chain of studies lengthens, quantitative data vis-à-vis qualitative data may grow in proportion and importance. Consequently, the terms *exploration* and *exploratory research* subsume both forms of data, whatever their ratio and significance in any one study in the chain of studies or in the entire chain itself.

It is possible to conceive of concatenated exploration as a type of longitudinal research, although one rarely discussed in standard treatments of such research. From the foregoing definition, it is clear that concatenated exploration differs from, for example, longitudinal panel studies or trend studies of particular groups or some other phenomenon. The essence of this facet of exploration lies in its continuous interstudy comparisons of groups, activities, or processes. In principle, these studies could be carried out simultaneously, were it not for two procedural matters: Concatenated exploration is commonly conducted by a lone, albeit enthusiastic, pioneer, and data collection in a given study is based to some extent on leads suggested by certain findings from studies carried out earlier in the chain.

It is noteworthy that most exploratory sociologists have been noticeably less inclined than their counterparts in anthropology to stay with a research subject through several rounds of fieldwork, analysis, and publication. These sociologists typically conduct one or two field projects, which may or may not be related, then retire to their offices to write empirical elaborations of their data, theoretical and methodological expositions, upper-division textbooks in their speciality, and even personal memoirs. The result is that scientific understanding of an area of social life that has been given a good start through exploratory research is, because of neglect, commonly arrested thereafter. For it is rare that someone else takes up the project where the pioneering researcher left off. In significant part, this is a question of personal lifestyle, a matter addressed in greater detail in Chapter 5.

Nevertheless, exceptions to this indictment do exist, a few of which should be mentioned to demonstrate that concatenated exploration is not only desirable but also possible. One collection of experiences in the field (Shaffir & Stebbins, 1991) contains a small number of examples, each consisting of a short description with bibliographic references. There, it is noted that Robert G. Burgess spent more than 20 years conducting a variety of interrelated studies on different phases of British education, ranging from nursery school through primary and secondary school to university and adult education. William B. Shaffir, since his graduate school days in the late 1960s, has been examining various aspects of community life among orthodox Jews in Canada and Israel. Steven J. Taylor, at times in collaboration with Robert Bogdan, explored the social world of the mentally retarded in the United States. They launched their first research project in this area in 1972. My own studies of amateurs and professionals in art, sci-

14

ence, sport, and entertainment (which began in 1973) also exemplify this genre of research.

On the whole, however, the enthusiasm among social scientists for concatenated exploration remains as weak today as it was in 1976, when John Lofland (1976) wrote,

> Qualitative strategy analysts have published relatively little to indicate concern with how their inquiries might cumulate or be consolidated into larger wholes. Each of their studies tends to be, rather, an individual cameo, a pretty thing standing more or less alone. Each is, of course, informed by a shared perspective... but not by any strict sense of programed, specific contribution to an existing and clearly articulated "theory." ...
>
> To my knowledge, no one has yet completed a consolidating effort with the features just enumerated. (pp. 91-92)

Part of the problem, Lofland concluded, was a dearth of studies that could be consolidated in this manner. Unfortunately, this lack shows no signs of disappearing.

When a social scientist devotes many years to exploring a related set of groups, processes, or activities, it is inevitable that the methodological and theoretical foundations of his or her research will undergo significant change. The specific nature of that change is, to be sure, always closely aligned with the subject under study, making it, on the whole, an idiosyncratic transformation. Its general direction is, nevertheless, possible to identify and describe, as has been done schematically in Figure 1. The first two columns of this figure bear most closely on the present discussion.

As data accumulate across the chain of exploratory studies, the grounded theory emerging from them grows in detail, breadth, and validity. Indeed, an evolving substantive grounded theory may have applicability broad enough to warrant elaborating it into a formal grounded theory (Glaser & Strauss, 1967, Chapter 4). Whatever happens, generic concepts (Couch, 1984; Prus, 1987) are also developed; they help bridge specific research settings and samples of subjects. With the concatenation of field studies, there is a tendency for exploration to be increasingly channeled by the developing conceptual framework, sometimes aided at the data collection level by semi-structured or, more rarely, fully structured measuring instruments. In the study of partially known phenomena (middle column of Figure 1), inductive discovery mixes at times with a certain amount of deductive prediction made possible by the emerging theory.

In short, qualitative researchers engaged in concatenated exploration gradually move away from the ideal typical model of exploratory data collection, analysis, and writing toward an intermediate model that also bears some resemblance to the ideal-typical model of confirmatory data collection, analysis, and writing. Still, to the extent that the four projects just mentioned can be regarded as presently operating more or less within the intermediate model, they provide, through their authors' accounts of their field experiences, evidence for the observation that reasonably open exploration continues, at least for the moment, to be a dominant procedure in the investigation of each new related group, activity, or social process (see Shaffir & Stebbins, 1991).

As the field of study advances toward the middle column of Figure 1 and beyond to the third column, there may also be a tendency to frame parts of the grounded theory that have been emerging in one or more established—although, at best, only partially grounded—theory groups in the social sciences. Qualitative sociologists seem most inclined to accomplish this by organizing and interpreting their work according to the symbolic interactionist school of thought. But other microperspectives can also be used (e.g., exchange theory), as can various macroperspectives such as neo-institutional theory, network theory, and political economy. One canon of exploratory research, however, is that framing grounded theory within an established theory group must be done so that it avoids constraining as much as possible the exploratory process itself (see Chapter 4).

Received theory, because it is inevitably limited in scope, has a way of more narrowly channeling data collection than is desirable at a time when discovery is still a main research goal. Received theory may also dominate to the point where the people who were studied appear in the research report as "automated figures who are pushed and pulled according to whatever theoretical scheme animates the tale" (Van Maanen, 1988, p. 131). But established theoretical frameworks can be of help during the analysis and writing stages of particular research projects in organizing and interpreting exploratory data, especially those coming later in the chain of studies where the grounded theory is now reasonably well elaborated.

ADVANTAGES OF CONCATENATION

One distinct advantage of concatenated exploration is that it serves to refute the charge that qualitative research consists chiefly of ungeneralizable case studies. The preceding discussion of its methodological and theoretical foundations indicates that a chain of qualitative case studies steadily expands the range of applicability as well as the level of validity of the accumulating findings from each component field investigation. Otherwise, exploration is subject, sometimes rightly so, to the charge of pandering to an entertainment-seeking public with "cute" studies of seemingly scientifically trivial phenomena such as Santa Claus and the telephone (Ball, 1968; Hagstrom, 1966).

A second advantage of concatenated exploration is that it capitalizes on the cumulative expertise of those who do it. As they continue to work with the groups, activities, or social processes of interest to them, they learn the ropes: how to enter the field with minimal effort and disruption of subjects, how to avoid procedural and interpersonal problems once on the inside, how to interview people there with greatest effectiveness, and how to leave the field and maintain relations with it in the future. Having developed an understanding of the social life of one setting, these qualitative researchers often have a head start in understanding that of analogous settings. In short, those who concatenate their exploratory studies need not start from scratch with each new project, as would be necessary for someone unfamiliar with the research area.

The third advantage stems from the remarks of Carl Couch (1991) in a book review. Couch noted that many qualitative researchers, because they focus chiefly on individuals, neglect either to study the social processes and relationships in which those individuals live or to put these matters in comparative perspective. Longitudinal exploration of a set of related groups or social processes helps correct such oversights by forcing researchers to recognize and compare these two basic sociological elements of human life.

To be counted as still another advantage is the fact that concatenated exploration lends itself especially well to team research. Such research profits from the discoveries of two or more investigators and their diverse perspectives (every field researcher sees the field somewhat differently), while facilitating development of a community of scholars around a common interest, namely, the overall project. Graduate students may also collaborate with a team of exploratory researchers, not as mere assistants or secondary analysts of someone else's data but as full-fledged members who, through their own studies, make valuable and distinctive contributions in their own name. These students, to the extent they contribute to a concatenated project, also help extend it into the next generation of scientists.

An important strength of concatenated exploration is the opportunity it creates for qualitative researchers to push the study of sets of related groups, activities, or social processes toward increased methodological and theoretical rigor (both qualitative and quantitative) to the extent allowed by the development of their grounded theories. As on-site overseers of the larger project, as it were, they are not inclined to jump to premature theoretical closure or premature methodological sophistication, in the sense that they would terminate exploration when it is still needed. Outsiders to the chain of studies in question are unlikely to have this insight and, without it, are likely to commit precisely this error.

Conclusions

Although qualitative methods are catching on these days among younger generations of social scientists and exploration is a more familiar word to them, no evidence exists in these circles of an exceptional commitment to concatenation vis-à-vis their older colleagues, many of whom are wont to retire from active fieldwork after one or two projects. Granted, a couple of explorations are unquestionably better than none at all, but many of the problems discussed in this chapter will remain unsolved if longer term concatenation is abjured on a wide scale. Just as bad, as will be noted later, many of the personal advantages that come with a life devoted to scientific exploration will be missed. In good part, then, what would-be social science explorers need to get them hooked on exploration, both as process and as lifestyle, is a sense of how profoundly satisfying it can actually be. Once deep satisfaction is found in research, concatenation becomes more appealing, for the researcher is now a true *amator* of his or her work. Because amateurs love what they are doing, they have little trouble becoming motivated to do it. And, happily, professionals can also be amateurs in this sense (Stebbins, 1992a, pp. 43-45).

2. EXPLORING

Exploration in the social sciences has, on occasion, been pejoratively described as a mere "fishing expedition." Such a metaphor calls up images of researchers randomly casting about for new generalizations, a procedure that, to the extent anyone actually follows it, is more akin to serendipity than to exploration. Indeed, the only difference between scientific fishing and scientific serendipity is that the latter is passive, whereas the former is active (oh yes, the catch is different, too). Obviously, as a metaphor for exploration, the fishing trip leaves much to be desired.

A much more appropriate metaphor for illuminating the process of exploration is setting and realizing an agenda for a meeting. Agendas are normally established in advance of the get-together and consist of a number of points to be considered there, each of which can potentially generate discussion and new ideas not previously weighed. The convention of proceeding late in the agenda to the point called *varia* is tantamount to another way of searching for new ideas, for items not thought of when the agenda was being created. "Business arising" can be seen in this metaphor as relating the present research to past projects in the same area, as a way of advancing concatenation, whereas minutes of previous meetings are equivalent to research reports of previous studies in the chain. The meeting metaphor breaks down, however, when certain technical aspects of running meetings are added to the basic image, such as rules of procedure, points of order, and motions to table. As necessary as these may be for the effective and efficient running of meetings, they nevertheless constrain free-wheeling exploration (and give-and-take in meetings), showing dramatically the limitations of this metaphor.

Still, the meeting metaphor does clearly make the point that scientific exploration does have some structure, best described as a set of broad *guidelines* suggesting what to look for and where to look for it. That exploration is guided rather than legislated follows from the requirement that the group, process, activity, or situation under study be systematically examined in a flexible and open-minded fashion.

Setting the Agenda

Social scientists set their exploratory research agendas in various ways, three of which are considered here. They draw on selected aspects of general social science theory, elaborate new central concepts, or, on a preliminary basis, directly observe or read about the group, process, activity, or situation. Some agendas are formed by combining two or even all three of these.

GENERAL THEORY

Exploratory researchers are frequently enjoined to enter their area of study purged of all conceptualizations acquired in their past that might slant the present collection and interpretation of data. Generally speaking, this is a good idea, but these explorers must still be careful not to throw the baby out with the bath water. Basic social science concepts do abound that can help guide and expand exploration, while posing no significant threat of contamination to the collection and interpretation of data.

For example, sociologists and anthropologists know that people everywhere in the world occupy certain statuses, in line with which they enact certain roles. In exploring a new area of social life, these two pillars of social science theory direct trained researchers to look for local expressions of them. Thus, armed though he was with his general knowledge of statuses and roles, Gary Fine (1998) could still discover, only through exploration, that amateur mushroomers "see the world as divided into mycophiles and mycophobes. Some understand the natural world well enough to appreciate its bounty, whereas others choose to remain ignorant" (pp. 206-212). A similar process of local specification occurs with reference to such time-worn concepts as group, lifestyle, community, social network, and personal and social identity. The list is long. An exploratory researcher not trained in these components of social theory, compared with those who are, would not be as attuned to them and, while in the field, would therefore likely fail to observe at least some of them.

Blumer (1969, pp. 146-152) referred to these guiding ideas as *sensitizing concepts,* and more recently, Van den Hoonaard (1997) has deemed them important enough for social science research to devote a small book to discussing them. The latter writes that other concepts, elaborated outside general theory, also serve to sensitize researchers about where to explore for new data and ideas. I have grouped these under the heading of defined concepts.

DEFINED CONCEPTS

An especially vexing feature of some forms of exploration is that, although the aim is usual—to learn all that is important about a given subject (group, activity, process, situation)—the subject itself may be poorly defined. At times, it is possible to solve this problem by examining not only the central subject but also some of its marginal expressions. At other times, however, to do this would make the project too unwieldy. To avoid the problems of unwieldiness and infinite regress, various cutting points may have to be established, something achieved in part by defining more crisply the principal subject of study.

I have faced this problem on numerous occasions. In my study of stand-up comics and their art, for instance, I learned early that confusion existed everywhere about the scope of these two (Stebbins, 1990, pp. 4-5). Does stand-up include sketch, mime, clowning, or team comedy? At the time, both dictionary and industry definitions were vague, with some encompassing all these forms. Yet studying the lot would have been a Herculean job. After examining the essence of each theatrical form, I found it evident that stand-up could be classified as a separate type of variety comedy, definable as the art of humorous commentary presented in a spontaneously conversational manner, typically by one person, before an audience. Multiple-person comedy teams, sketch groups included, perform in a significantly different way (using props, scripts, etc.) as do quasi-comedic storytellers, satirists, and ethical monologuists. Mixed stand-up comedy combines oral and sensory humor, the stock-in-trade of many a mime, clown, and entertainment magician. Improvisational theater was also excluded, because it involves spontaneous acting, unlike stand-up, which is preplanned. Each of these is a distinctive art, I discovered, and therefore merits being studied in its own right. With the definitional problem solved in this manner, the study of stand-up could then proceed.

Stand-up comics and stand-up comedy are, at bottom, commonsense conceptions of a well-known type of entertainment artist and the activity in which he or she engages. Other instances of this kind of preliminary defining of commonsense concepts are scattered throughout the social science literature. Erving Goffman (1967, pp. 47-112), for example, devoted a significant part of his career to this sort of intellectual enterprise, as seen in his studies of deference, demeanor, and embarrassment. Likewise, Clanton and Smith (1977) faced similar definitional hurdles in their study of jealousy, as did Ball (1965) when he set out to examine sarcasm. And I encountered this challenge at the beginning of my work on amateurs (Stebbins, 1979).

At times, however, the concept to be studied lies outside the commonsense world; it is a scientific idea about which the general public has scant knowledge and on which even the best unabridged dictionaries shed little or no light. Some of these concepts can also be fuzzy, despite having been born in a scientific milieu. Moreover, vague or not, every specialized scientific term was coined by someone, suggesting that, heretofore, a term for the phenomenon that the coiner and researcher intended to explore was not even in the science's lexicon. Whether the concept is a fuzzy but established one or a clear but newly elaborated one, the reasons just given for sharpening definitions of commonsense concepts apply with equal validity to these more esoteric ideas.

Goffman, off and on over his career, found himself in precisely this situation. For instance, he had first to invent and define the term *frame* (the way people organize their personal experiences in particular social situations) before he could carry out his several frame analyses (Goffman, 1974, pp. 1-14). Csikszentmihalyi (1975, pp. xi-xiii) had basically defined the psychological process of "flow" before he launched his longitudinal study of it, even though the word itself was adopted only later, after his subjects repeatedly mentioned it. They frequently employed the word *flow* to describe their feelings when fully absorbed in challenging and captivating work or leisure, activity they nonetheless felt capable of executing. I found the concept of definition of the situation (the meaning people give to social situations before they act with reference to them) in such definitional disarray that it was necessary to sharpen its meaning prior to conducting exploratory research on its use among classroom teachers (Stebbins, 1975, Chapters 1-2). I did not invent this term, however; W. I. Thomas coined it, possibly writing about it as early as 1917 (Volkart, 1951, Introduction).

WHAT TO EXPLORE

The idea of spatial exploration might suggest to some readers that people who explore do this on a grand scale, as in exploring the New World, the moon, or the Arctic sea. But in fact, social science exploration can be of almost any scope. Examples given to this point have already conveyed a sense of this; teachers' definitions of a particular type of classroom situation (e.g., disorderly behavior, being tardy) and people's experience of flow in a particular activity have narrower scope than the social worlds of mushroomers and stand-up comics.

Narrower still are the growing number of quantitative procedures designed to be executed in the exploration phase of the scientific process, many of which can be classified as either exploratory data analysis or exploratory factor analysis. The first refers to a bundle of methods developed by John Tukey for discovering new patterns and relationships wherein quantitative data are visually represented, as in the well-known "stem-and-leaf" display and "box-and-whisker" diagram. The veins in the leaf and the whiskers projecting from the box represent the new patterns and relationships sought in this special kind of exploration. As in the studies of flow and definition of the situation, where exploration is circumscribed by the two central concepts being studied, exploration in these two forms of analysis is circumscribed by the data that have been gathered for the analysis.

This holds as well for exploratory factor analysis, during which the analyst strives to discover the latent or hidden variables underlying a set of manifest variables or measures, that is, those known to the researcher. Thus, Hunter and Manley (1986) used this statistical technique to search for the variables underlying 43 categories of functions that workers in Canada have been shown to perform in several thousand occupations. Their exploratory factor analysis revealed eight latent factors that, together, summarize these

22

functions. They discovered, for instance, that one of these factors, cognitive complexity of an occupation (e.g., level of knowledge, abstractness of knowledge) was positively related to the manifest variable of occupational status. They found, however, that another factor—level of responsibility in the occupation—was not at all related to its status in the community.

Explorations using narratives and case studies, a common practice in discovery research in, among other fields, nursing and social work, tend to be narrow, compared with the ethnographic exploration of, say, sociologists and anthropologists. Let us call the former *personality-centered research*. It contrasts with the latter, or *community-centered research,* which examines larger pieces of social life, such as certain roles and their interface, workings of an entire community, social worlds of particular groups, and lifestyles associated with various occupations. *Language-centered research,* research in linguistics and conversation analysis, is also narrow and, in this sense, is much like personality-centered research. Still, all exploration is limited to some extent, for no researcher can study everything at once. As stated earlier, I decided to examine only stand-up comics, leaving for another time or another investigator the exploration of clowns, sketch artists, and improvisional actors.

HOW TO EXPLORE

A general answer to the question of how to explore has already been given: The explorer searches for generalizations leading to a detailed and profound understanding of the group, process, or activity under study. But what does this advice mean in concrete terms? One, it means explorers look for such generalizations along lines suggested by relevant sensitizing concepts. Two, in exploring through observation, observers literally attend as much as possible to all that is going on, trying in this way to note recurrent phenomena deemed important in their science, according to certain sensitizing concepts (e.g., patterns of thought, belief, behavior) and according to the talk and actions of people they are examining. Exploration using interviews is more focused than exploration based on observation, primarily because the first commonly employs an interview guide, many items of which are suggested by preliminary observation and by the contents of documents written by or about those people. And sometimes, depending on the object of study, researchers can also learn about it by examining life records (e.g., letters, diaries, biographies) and archival sources (e.g., church records, newspaper articles, government statistics) as well as by using a variety of nonreactive measures such as visible patterns of use or wear of objects or amounts and kinds of discarded goods (Webb, Campbell, Schwartz, Sechrest, & Grove, 1981).

Three, I have responded to student queries about how to explore by stating that researchers, probably more often unaware than not, look for the five Ws. They try to generalize about *who* is doing (thinking, feeling) *what* to (with, for, about) *whom* and *when* and *where* this action is taking place. My experience in the field suggests, however, that this little formula is more heuristic than practical. At least I can never recall consciously invoking the five Ws as a way of directing my observations or helping me think up items for an interview guide. Yet, in great part, my findings could be classified according to them. In fact, the five Ws are but a more particular, and I would argue workable, expression of Glaser's (1978) advice that exploration be conducted by searching for "categories" (of whos, whats, etc.) as well as for a special category he calls "basic social processes."

Setting out the five Ws is as far as I have been willing to go in training people for exploration in the social sciences. C. Wright Mills (1959), in his appendix on "intellectual craftsmanship," explains why this is a good point at which to draw the line on formulas:

> Perhaps he [the technician] is too well trained, too precisely trained. Since one can be *trained* only in what is already known, training sometimes incapacitates one from learning new ways; it makes one rebel against what is bound to be at first loose and even sloppy. But you must cling to such vague images and notions, if they are yours, and you must work them out. For it is in such forms that original ideas, if any, almost always first appear. (p. 212)

Exploration is no place for data collection formulas distilled from conventional theory and methodological practice. On the contrary, exploration is where the art of science is most widely exercised, the area of science where imagination reigns most freely. Creativity in this domain comes through inductive reasoning, as researchers discover order in what initially appeared to them as chaos.

Mills's little appendix is a veritable gold mine of ideas about how to explore. For example, he urges researchers to establish a file on each project they intend to carry out and to do this immediately on deciding that in the future, no matter how distant, the project will actually be undertaken. Meanwhile, fill the file at will with random ideas about the subject of research and with newspaper and magazine clippings and notes from scholarly books and articles that bear on it. Brochures, television and radio documentaries, and snippets of conversations with people constitute the same order of material; references to them should also be placed in the file. Besides suggesting answers to the five Ws, answers otherwise sought in the interviews and observations, it may be possible to incorporate some of the contents of the file in the study's written form. At this time, Mills observed, these materials can often be juxtaposed to generate new ideas born of the contrasts that sometimes appear. This is the "sociological imagination" at work.

Three other points in Mills's appendix merit consideration in this section. First, a person can explore by playing with words and phrases, accomplished by going to an unabridged dictionary and reading the different senses in the definitions of key words and then following up related terms to see how they are defined. In this way, I learned a great deal about the idea of amateur, pursuing references in the dictionary definitions of this type to entries on professional, dilettante, amateurish, and the like. Second, Mills notes that insights can sometimes be gained by contemplating phenomena in their extremes or as opposites. If, for example, despair is a relevant emotion, then what about elation; if poverty is a relevant condition, then what about wealth? Third, never forget history. I now counsel all my students to devote at least a chapter of their thesis to the historical background of the group, process, activity, or situation they are studying. Somehow, earlier in my career, I forgot Mills's advice in this regard and, for many years, produced ahistorical studies in deviance, education, and leisure. I finally discovered this oversight in the study of entertainment magicians (Stebbins, 1993b), mainly because my research subjects talked so excitedly about great magicians and magical acts of the past that I could hardly escape their importance.

The foregoing portrayal of exploration as like the setting of an agenda and the subsequent argument for a predominantly nonformulaic approach to learning how to explore raises several prickly questions about its real value in the social sciences. One of these revolves around the role of induction in these disciplines.

Induction, Deduction, and Exploration

Kaplan (1964, pp. 13-18), in an all too short section on discovery, expressed his belief that there is a logic to scientific intuition, that discovery is more than mere chance, mere serendipity: "There is surely a basic difference between intuition and guesswork—between intuition of the great creative genius or even of the ordinary experienced scientific worker, and the complete novice's blind, blundering guesswork or mechanical trial and error" (p. 14). Although Kaplan failed to describe in concrete terms this difference, the preceding discussion indicates that it lies in the process of exploration, the intellectual foundation of which is inductive reasoning. Kaplan did, however, claim that the logic of intuition "should concern itself with the process of scientific discovery, with the process of reaching conclusions as well as with the proof of the conclusions reached" (p. 17).

But do the generalizations emerging from exploratory data really constitute proof of the validity of those generalizations? The answer to this question, although still debated from time to time in philosophical circles (Lacey, 1986, pp. 94-97), is, among contemporary social scientists, negative. Glaser and Strauss (1967), for example, are unequivocal on this issue everywhere in their book: Exploration produces hypotheses, tentative generalizations about the group, process, activity, or situation being studied. These hypotheses, they argue, must eventually be verified, as when they are tested in a research design expressly created for this purpose. In other words, it is logically impossible to generate and confirm hypotheses using the same data.

Of course, if an exploration is competently carried out, it is highly improbable that generalizations emerging from it will be falsified in subsequent attempts to verify them on the same sample of subjects and activities. Because of the grounded validity of the data in this situation, their verification using the same sample, although technically required, would turn out to be old news. But, in fact, few if any confirmatory studies working with exploratory generalizations are carried out on the same sample. Much more commonly, a new, albeit related sample is selected, say, in a similar activity, another organization, a distant part of the country, or a different ethnic minority. In effect, such studies aim both to test some of the generalizations that have come down from earlier explorations and to extend the scope of the ever-emerging grounded theory.

If the principle of induction is easy enough for social scientists to grasp, many of them find more elusive some of its ramifications. Trained, as the majority are, in deductive theory and confirmatory procedures, they are inclined to evaluate exploratory generalizations from these standpoints. In particular, they are moved to question the reliability and validity of these generalizations. Validity in exploration centers on the need to gain an accurate or true impression of the phenomenon under study. Reliability refers to replicability, to whether another researcher with similar methodological training, understanding of the research setting, and rapport with its members can make similar observations.

It is not my intent to go into detail in this chapter about these two issues, which are real in exploration, on which many pages have already been written (e.g., Altheide & Johnson, 1994, Chapter 30; Katz, 1983, pp. 139-144) and to which I will return in Chapter 4. Three points about them befitting the scope of the present book are, however, not to be missed at this point. One, validity in exploration is, in at least one way, substantially different from that in confirmation. In the first, concern lies with the explorer's capacity to acquire directly an accurate impression of a group, process, activity, or situation, whereas in the second, concern lies with the investigator's capacity to find measures and indices that indirectly convey an accurate impression of these phenomena. In fact, compared with confirmation validity, exploration validity is more easily resolved, for example, by using different methods to examine the same group or activity (known as triangulation), asking key informants to comment on the familiarity and reasonableness of observations, and finding recurrent evidence for each generalization. Unfortunately, confirmatory researchers sometimes have to evaluate exploratory work, even though they are accustomed to working only with indirect measures and often know little about how validity is achieved and assessed in the realm of discovery. In this situation, they are wont to try to force the exploratory study into the Procrustean bed of verification validation.

Two, confirmatory researchers are also inclined to use what might be called a one-shot approach to assessing both validity and reliability: Each study undertaken must meet established criteria on both accounts. By contrast, exploratory researchers, to the extent they concatenate their research, take a more global approach, arguing that judgments about validity and reliability are to be made with reference to a set of studies, which together demonstrate most convincingly how these two conditions have been realized. Although validity and reliability are also important to them in each study they execute, exploratory researchers recognize that the most authoritative statement about validity and reliability can only be made down the road in the wake of several open-ended investigations.

Three, validity in exploration has a lot to do with representativeness of the sample of groups, processes, or activities being examined. Validity is strongest when hypothetical generalizations emerge from direct empirical study of a set of representative instances. If, for example, a study purports to be an exploration of everyday life in the primary school classrooms in a particular city and every primary school there is observed, then representativeness of that sample is assured by means of this 100% coverage. But were the private schools or the schools in a certain district of the city omitted from the study, this claim to representativeness would be false and the validity of the project, for this reason, impugned.

Representativeness can be achieved in a number of ways, including random-sampling lists of people, drawing samples in such a way that they include instances of all relevant factors (purposive sampling), and using snowball procedures to recruit research subjects (the investigator asks subjects to identify people who might agree to participate in the study). Choosing one of these depends on how the group, process, activity, or situation under consideration is organized. Whatever the situation, seasoned explorers invariably spend a good deal of time on this matter, and in my experience, graduate thesis examining committees and reviewers of scholarly manuscripts submitted for publication show an abiding interest in it as well. This having been said, sample representativeness in an exploratory study is usually less than perfect, mainly because perfection on this matter is often an impossible goal. Inadequate representativeness thus becomes another incitement to concatenate research studies in a particular area and to treat the question of validity as a condition to reckon with throughout the chain. The problem of sample representativeness is considered in detail in the five vignettes reported in the next chapter.

In the meantime, while on the subject of validity and representativeness, we should also consider the frequently asked question of how large a sample should be, however representative. The conventional answer is that researchers sample in exploration until "theoretical saturation" is reached and "no additional data are being found whereby the . . . [social scientist] can develop properties of the category" (Glaser & Strauss, 1967, p. 61). But this advice pertains to data collection, not to subsequent data analysis. To ensure adequate numbers for the latter process, my working rule over the years has always been to try to observe or interview a minimum of 30 people per group, process, activity, or situation studied. If, for example, two groups are being compared, then the overall sample should, if at all possible, be at least 60 (see also Morse, 1994, p. 225).

Why 30 cases per unit of investigation? Because it is important to allow for the emergence of important categories and subcategories that will inevitably occur during the study; these are among the critical differences in how the group, process, activity, or situation operates or unfolds in routine circumstances. Moreover, these categories must have enough cases—four or five at minimum—to constitute a foundation for valid exploratory generalizations. Thus, in the study of entertainment magicians, I soon learned that its female practitioners meet with special problems in a profession historically dominated by males and that I would therefore have to make a special effort to find and interview the former. Were my sample of all magicians too small, I would have run the risk of having too few women from which to generalize about them. All this has come by way of experience: I tried samples of 25 in the study of amateur actors, archaeologists, and baseball players but found the samples too small. I have used 30 ever since, and to good effect.

By the way, this advice about 30 cases for analytic purposes does not apply very well to personality-centered research, where respondents are interviewed on several occasions and, as already mentioned, analysis centers on more or less whole personalities. Research here is more labor intensive than the community-centered variety, typically being conducted with smaller samples of sometimes no more than 10 or 12 cases (see third vignette in Chapter 3). Unfortunately, I am unaware of any recommended minimum sample size for this kind of exploration, although I do frequently encounter studies based on 10 to 12 cases. Riessman (1993) says only that "more than one case study is essential if we want to show variation. To reach theoretical levels of abstraction, comparative work is desirable" (p. 70). Lieblich, Tuval-Mashiach, and Zilber (1998) are no more precise, observing generally that "most narrative studies are conducted with smaller groups of individuals than the sample size employed in traditional research" (p. 9).

Qualitative and Quantitative

Despite the fact that, in much of exploratory research, social scientists collect both qualitative and quantitative data, those who work in this part of their discipline have come to be known more specifically as *qualitative researchers,* as men and women who pursue, for example, qualitative sociology or psychology. This discrepancy between the nature of research data and the popular identification of researchers has misled some newcomers to exploration by implying that quantitative data of any kind have no place in qualitative social science and hence no place in exploration. Nevertheless, most scholars who routinely explore soon learn from the literature on the subject and their own experience that adjectives such as *qualitative* and *interpretive* refer to a methodological approach—to exploration—rather than to the nature of the data collected under the aegis of that approach. Note, moreover, that in everyday social science parlance, usage of the term *qualitative* is even more complicated than this, because it also describes research that relies primarily on qualitative data to confirm hypotheses. But because this book centers on the exploratory zone of the exploration-confirmation continuum, qualitative researchers operating outside it will not be considered.

It is difficult to know precisely when the qualitative-quantitative distinction took root in the social sciences or from where it came or who invented it. For a long time, it was unnecessary to distinguish the two approaches, because empirical work in social sciences was chiefly descriptive, and theory was predominantly of the armchair variety. Research in the early days of these disciplines, when it occurred, was mainly qualitative and exploratory, even if it was rarely, if ever, described in these terms.

Perhaps the two ideas were borrowed from chemistry, which has long distinguished between qualitative and quantitative analyses of constituents present in a substance. Whatever its provenance, Glaser and Strauss (1967, pp. 15-18) observe in their discussion of the distinction that it gradually became current in sociology during the period running from the late 1930s to the early 1950s, a time in that discipline when quantification and measurement were gaining considerable ground. The distinction between nominal and ordinal levels of (qualitative) measurement, on the one hand, and ratio and interval levels of (quantitative) measurement, on the other, also helped to further define the separate territory of the two approaches. Moreover, as Van Maanen (1998, p. xix) speculates for organizational studies, colleges and universities in Canada and the United States from the mid-1960s through the 1970s experienced a growth spurt in the number of students and professors credited to their name. In place of old-fashioned theory building, newfangled theory testing seems to have become popular, an attitude that lent itself well to a life in research using recently expanded computer facilities and the latest quantitative techniques. Finally, the rise of quantitative research brought with it the need to pretest measuring instruments and conduct pilot studies to iron out kinks in procedure and sharpen precision so the main study could proceed as flawlessly as possible. Some social scientists viewed, and still view, exploration as synonymous with these preliminary steps, as mere rehearsal for the big show, so to speak.

The foregoing indicates that referring to research as qualitative is not the most accurate nomenclature for identifying exploration in the social sciences. But, alas, *qualitative research, qualitative researcher,* and their various derivatives have gained ascendancy as terms of choice. To insist on linguistic purity at this point in the name of greater precision of communication is pointless, possibly even self-defeating. Indeed, a main goal of this book is to flesh out the idea of exploration and link it with that of exploratory qualitative research to show that the two are the same and to enrich understanding of both.

Conclusions

It has been necessary to treat the various points made in this chapter in significant part because a widespread tendency prevails in the social sciences to regard research problems of all kinds—whether they require exploration or not—through the prism of confirmatory research, the research approach in which the vast majority of social scientists are trained. Even if they can accept the argument that, when little is known scientifically about a group, process, activity, or situation, it is better to explore and generate hypotheses than try to test hypotheses derived from hunches or distant received theory, many of them seem to have difficulty following the ramifications of this principle. It is these scholars who, when faced with exploratory work, are likely to insist on evaluating its validity and reliability from a confirmatory perspective or to resort to inappropriate formulas such as applying inferential statistical tests to the data, even though there is, in fact, nothing to infer.

As will be argued in more detail in Chapter 5, exploration is, among other things, a state of mind, a special personal orientation toward data collection, analysis, and writing. Would-be explorers in the social sciences who come from confirmatory backgrounds, an increasingly common occurrence these days, must learn when to bracket their earlier training and take the mantle of discovery. Otherwise, they will fail to effectuate true exploration or, at best, will be only partially successful in their attempt.

Before proceeding to the chapters on writing exploratory research and the lifestyle of the researcher devoted to this approach, I offer an interlude of examples that demonstrate some of the different subjects that can be explored and how researchers go about doing this.

3. EXPLORATION ILLUSTRATED

Although professional researchers have produced a great variety of exploratory studies in a growing number of social science disciplines, here I have decided to illustrate various aspects of the process of exploration, as depicted in both earlier and subsequent chapters of this book, with projects undertaken by some of the master's and doctoral students with whom I have worked over the years. One reason for this restriction is to show first-timers in this genre of research that they, too, can do it; exploration is not solely the province of seasoned, degree-holding social scientists. Another reason is that, quite frankly, I am unable to keep abreast of the ever-expanding qualitative literature coming out of the burgeoning list of disciplines in which exploratory research is being conducted these days. Of course, I came to know reasonably well the specialized areas in which my students were working. That much was relatively easy. Far more difficult, however, is gaining knowledge of the qualitative work carried out in the nine disciplines in which I have been involved (see Introduction), knowledge that would be sufficient to enable me to identify in each a decently representative exemplar of exploration.

Five vignettes are presented here, each serving as a brief report on a thesis written in a different discipline. The first two theses, written in sociology and psychology, are of the standard variety, in that their authors tackle research problems that emerged in relation to the literature of their disciplines. The next two, which were done in nursing and community health science, exemplify studies undertaken to explore a certain practical problem in the local community. The fifth thesis was written in the field of environmental design; it is an evaluation, a practical problem of a special sort.

I open each vignette with a description of the research problem the student elected to tackle. This leads to the question of why he or she chose exploration rather than verification. Next, I explain how the student dealt with the sampling problem. A brief discussion of data collection techniques follows. The vignettes end with a statement about some of the study's main findings and their theoretical and practical import. Using these five projects as a springboard, the concluding section of the chapter examines questions of generalizability and conclusiveness in exploratory research.

Middle-Class Marijuana Users and Lifestyle

Andrew Hathaway (1995) found, while reviewing the sociological literature on marijuana consumption for his master's thesis, that research on lifestyles of users of this drug was next to nonexistent. Considering the idea of lifestyle (a sensitizing concept in sociology) raises questions about the role this drug plays in the everyday lives of regular users. For after all, simple possession of marijuana is itself illegal (possession strictly for personal consumption), even if the law is only lightly enforced these days, which suggests that regular users must still exercise caution when acquiring and consuming it. Moreover, regular use implies that the person values this drug highly and is therefore prepared to live with its attendant social and legal risks.

Sociologists and psychologists, among others, have devoted considerable time to studying marijuana use, and in several areas of this speciality, confirmatory research is now and has been for many years the order of the day. Still, as happens in many of the "mature" fields in the social sciences, scattered unexplored questions persist, hidden away in the half-life of the speciality, where they beg for the kind of open-ended examination needed to launch, or perhaps relaunch, the concatenation process. Through his review of the literature, Hathaway came to realize that the lifestyle of middle-class users was just such a question.

What is more, research in this field, even while it ignores lifestyle, has been conducted primarily on samples of university students—always a handy resource for university-based scientists—or on samples of volunteers of low socioeconomic status, who are often induced with nominal cash incentives to participate in the research. Thus, Hathaway's decision to study nonstudent, middle-class users brought still another new angle to the sociological examination of marijuana use. Thirty regular middle-class users (15 male, 15 female) living in Calgary were interviewed using a semistructured interview guide. Regular use was defined as consuming marijuana at least once a month for a minimum of a year. Interviewees were found using the snowball method, as implemented through their networks of personal contacts. Of course, it is impossible to know how representative such a sample is, but under the circumstances, no other sampling procedure would have worked as well.

Hathaway found that his respondents avoided the risks of acquiring the drug that come with patronizing professional dealers, preferring instead to use personal, familiar, and hence relatively safe networks of supply. Moreover, he discovered that the moral implications of marijuana use have diminished substantially over the years, leading his interviewees to be somewhat more open about it than they once were. These middle-class users had also abandoned some of the subcultural values of their youth, explaining their present interest in the drug in practical terms; for instance, it provides a means of relaxation and a social occasion to be shared with like-minded friends. And some of Hathaway's respondents argued that, while engaged in certain complicated work and leisure activities, marijuana focuses their attention or gives them an enlightening alternative perspective.

What are the implications of this study? The main implication is that recent decades have seen a substantial increase in societal tolerance toward the consumption of marijuana, which has helped foster the lifestyle Hathaway explored with his subjects. This new tolerance is, however, inconsistent with present Canadian and American law regulating simple possession of this drug. Furthermore, whatever the level of public tolerance in the two countries, the political climate is such that politicians are highly unlikely at this point in time to enact legislation designed to decriminalize simple possession. Even the proposal for reducing severity of penalties for such possession that are presently on the books has so far met with unflagging governmental resistance. So far, two publications have resulted from this study (Hathaway, 1997a, 1997b).

Women and the Development
of Occupational Aspirations

Nancy Johnson Smith (1997) made two broad observations that, in turn, persuaded her to undertake doctoral research on the ways women develop their occupational aspirations. First, she noted that, despite the scientifically demonstrated equivalence between the sexes with respect to intelligence and general ability, North American women have not aspired historically to the same range and distribution of occupations as men. Second, research on achievement has, in the main, been undertaken by and centered mainly on men. Moreover, as researchers, these men have relied almost exclusively on quantitative methods to collect their data. True, a handful of theories about women's achievement have been formulated in recent years, but alas, they, like the theories constructed by the men, exemplify all too well the problem of syllogistic reasoning described in Chapter 1. That is, they have been constructed from data gathered in controlled research designs or from theoretical fragments pulled together from received perspectives, themselves rooted in the results of controlled research.

Smith found, thus, that women's voices in this matter had been ignored. Accordingly, she set out to obtain their stories or narratives: "[I want] to take a qualitative approach that seeks to conceptualize new ways of understanding women's achievement-related choices from their points of view, that is, the meanings that choice can have for women themselves" (Smith, 1997, p. 20). Operationally, her research goal was to use exploratory data to discover an overall story line, inductively pulled from their accounts of how they arrived at their present university majors and occupational aspirations, as well as to uncover individual variations in this overarching narrative.

To ensure sufficient diversity in her sample of 26 undergraduate women, Smith sought interviewees from traditional (humanities, fine arts) and nontraditional (physical sciences) majors, almost all of whom were attending full-time the University of Calgary. She recruited most of her respondents from classes in these two types of majors, where she first described the project and then called for volunteers. Additional interviewees were found through referrals from students whom she had just interviewed. By design, all participants in the study were between 20 and 23 years of age and had completed at least 2 years of university studies. This resulted in a reasonably representative sample of university women (using combined purposive and snowball sampling procedures), all at a stage in life when they could reflect on those aspects of their past of interest to the researcher, while naturally expressing their reflections in narrative form in the context of an open-ended interview.

Smith's findings included the following. During childhood, the respondents tended to fantasize about gender-traditional occupations such as teacher or ballerina, while being oriented by family expectations for achievement, especially as this related to university training. In their high school years, they were inclined to minimize educational matters, however, emphasizing instead such gender-traditional social and affiliative issues as bodily changes and comparisons between self and peers. As they prepared to leave high school, many of Smith's respondents became sensitive once again to the opinions and advice of others on what their aspirations should be, ignoring in the process their own educational and occupational goals. This resulted, in the typical case, in a loss of confidence and an increased sensitivity to gender-role expectations. The study does show, nevertheless, that at the university, these women began to get serious about their education and their lifelong aspirations, which helped them regain some of the self-confidence lost earlier. In other words, the advice and opinions of others became less important when they conflicted with what the women saw as an interesting and satisfying major. The women had become, or were in the process of becoming, important agents in shaping their own future, using their own social skills to adapt to the variety of circumstances encountered along the way.

A wide variety of implications flow from this examination of female occupational aspirations. For one, it shows that, on entering a university, women do not necessarily have to compromise important aspects of self to survive in higher education. Instead, they can develop coping strategies and take responsibility for piloting their own way in pursuit of their personal goals. The respondents pointed out that activities and relationships that support this orientation were of utmost importance to them. Sometimes, a sport, hobby, or part-time job had this effect; sometimes, support came from a peer, teacher, or parent. Smith's study makes it clear that young women can cultivate their own support system and that they should be encouraged to do exactly that. Finally, it must not be forgotten that, as a woman moves through life, her understanding of career-related issues changes. Researchers, theoreticians, and counselors must understand that a static model of this process is too simple and therefore highly inadequate. The tendency, once in a university, for each to become her own agent with regard to life's goals attests to the wisdom of this implication. To date, Smith has published papers from this investigation (Smith, 1996, in press).

Becoming a Mother: Experiencing the Postpartum Phenomenon

In a doctoral study undertaken in the field of nursing, Sarla Sethi (1994) sought to describe the postpartum experiences of first-time mothers as they went through the first 3 months with their newly born infants. Although research had been conducted on the physiologic and psychosocial processes affecting these mothers during the first 6 weeks following birth, their views of this period in their lives had remained unexplored. Furthermore, it was important to describe how women see the postpartum experience for a longer span of time, namely 3 months, because earlier research had demonstrated that resolution of the aforementioned processes requires far more than 6 weeks.

Exploration was justified, in this instance, by an absence of qualitative research on how first-time postpartum women define the first 3 months following delivery of their babies. The studies undertaken to this point had been objective in orientation, measuring quantitatively certain aspects of life, but doing so during only the first 6 weeks of this period and without considering the woman's understanding of what was happening to her in her own social environment. The gap in knowledge created by this limited approach is critical, for the tensions some women feel during the first 3 months can affect resolution of the physiologic and psychosocial processes.

Sethi collected narrative data from 15 mothers, 12 of whom had delivered babies for the first time and, for comparative purposes, 3 of whom had given birth at least once before. Using an open-ended interview guide to facilitate exploration, each mother was interviewed twice during the 3-month period. The sample was drawn from a population of low-risk postpartum women who had no serious medical and psychosocial problems before, during, or after birth of their babies. In particular, interviewees were selected from women under care of the Nursing Division of the Calgary Health Services. Because all postpartum women in the city have some contact with this service during the first 3 months after delivery, Sethi was able to purposively sample from a list of the entire population of them. To capture the range of variation in age, educational background, and socioeconomic status of the population of postpartum mothers, she selected her respondents equally from the six regions of the Calgary Health Services. In addition, all who were interviewed had to be at least 18 years of age and fluent in English. They also had to have a pregnancy that lasted between 38 and 42 weeks, to deliver a healthy baby weighing at least 2,500 grams, to live with the baby's father, and to have no previous history of depression or pathological fatigue.

Sethi found that following childbirth, the women were constantly experiencing transformations as they adapted to the needs of their infants and the changes in their own personalities. This process, she observed, is dialectical. In other words, the woman faces numerous contradictions at this time, such as being happy to be a mother but upset over the loss of freedom and autonomy that motherhood entails. The result is tension, which nonetheless tends to get resolved through some sort of intellectual reconstruction; in this instance, the cost of the relative loss of freedom is felt to be offset by the reward of being a mother.

Moreover, the 3-month postpartum period has two phases. In the initial weeks, each mother is consumed with giving herself fully to her newborn while starting to redefine herself as a mother. After about the 12th week, she starts to concentrate more fully on the redefinition process. Redefinition also occurs with reference to the woman's relationships with others and with reference to her professional goals. This complicated process also has its contradictions and tensions, which are, in the typical case, resolved with the passage of time.

Because nurses are often called on to care for postpartum women and newborn babies, Sethi recommends that nurses be instructed on the postpartum experiences of women as well as how these mothers interpret their experiences during the first 3 months of delivery. Furthermore, women's stories and narratives, such as those collected in this study, could be used to instruct nurses about the meaning and dialectical nature of postpartum life. Sethi recommends training of this sort for practicing nurses as well as for students in nursing programs. Additional findings from her study are available in Sethi (1995).

Health Care Coordination:
The Consumer's View

The doctoral research of Alexandra Harrison (1998) centered on the meaning of coordination of health care services to former patients who had been moved from acute care in a hospital to the Home Care Program of the Calgary Regional Health Authority (CRHA). With the twin aims of providing health care more effectively and with less cost than heretofore, the 17 regional health authorities in Alberta were established in 1994 to bring all formerly independent health organizations under one administrative umbrella. But is such care now being provided? Have these two goals been met? Harrison discovered that no comprehensive research had ever been conducted on this question, even though the Alberta system and similar systems elsewhere in Canada have been in place for some time. Her study examined the consumer's or former patient's perspective of the transitional experience of being moved from a hospital to home care: "Consumers' experiences, as much as the technical quality of care, will affect how they benefit from and evaluate the health care system" (Harrison, 1998, p. 3).

The absence of a comprehensive examination of any such system in Canada justified an exploratory approach. It would have made little sense to try to guess at the complex meanings the transitional experience had for former patients and, with this information, form hypotheses for controlled testing, say, with a questionnaire. Rather, it was better to explore in depth these meanings to ensure that no important aspect or dimension was overlooked and that grounded theory was generated for subsequent testing.

In the study itself, only short-term home care clients were sampled for interviewing. To have interviewed all home care clients would have made an unmanageably large project for one person. Also, the short-term clients are an important group, primarily because they constitute about 20% of all such clients while accounting for more than 50% of use of professional home care services. Moreover, the short-term clients, compared with their long-term counterparts, are more likely to reflect the rationale for regionalizing health care: to shift care from hospitals to the community. Finally, with the decreasing length of time that patients spend in hospitals, short-term clients are the home care population most likely to be discharged early.

The sample consisted of English-speaking clients who were willing as well as mentally and physically able to be interviewed. Otherwise, people with any kind of medical problem requiring short-term home care who were discharged from one of Calgary's acute care hospitals were eligible for the study. To this end, Harrison was able to obtain a list of all clients discharged from one of these hospitals and registered for short-term home care service. To ensure representativeness, she first prepared a letter that explained the study and asked for participation in it. This was then sent, over the course of a week, to all consumers referred for short-term home care from one of the city's acute care hospitals, each being located in a different home care area of the six administered by the CRHA. Except for those who refused or were disqualified from the study for one of the aforementioned reasons, all were interviewed, resulting in a sample of 33. The interviews, most of which were face-to-face but some of which had to be conducted over the telephone, constituted the primary method by which Harrison collected data for her study. All interviews consisted, in the main, of open-ended questions designed to elicit the broadest possible range of responses.

Respondents were asked to describe their experiences in moving from an acute care hospital to the CRHA Home Care Program. They were further asked to indicate which aspects of coordination were important to them, coordination having to do with effectiveness of links between components of the CRHA. These clients defined coordination in terms of cooperation, continuity, working together, and similar considerations. Moreover, they stressed repeatedly their own role in coordination, effected primarily through communication, monitoring their personal situation, managing their lives, and staying informed. In this regard, most maintained that their care had been reasonably well coordinated, an observation that Harrison validated using a number of independent measures. And nearly all believed they had been discharged from the hospital at the appropriate moment.

Harrison's study demonstrated, among other things, that consumers of health services can and should be consulted about organizational functioning that affects them. Their views can help inform the people responsible for managing the boundaries that separate sectors of a health system as well as help smooth the transition for clients who are forced to cross them. Her study also showed these people to be actively involved in ensuring that coordination is carried out in their interest. Some of the results from this project have been reported in Harrison, Pablo, and Verhoef (1999).

Prison Inmates in Wildlife Rehabilitation

After reading descriptions of two wildlife rehabilitation programs that had been running in the United States since the early 1980s, Jill Sorensen decided in 1994 to open one of her own in Calgary. The basic operating principle of these programs is that, under supervision of paid wildlife technicians, prison inmates volunteer their time to care for injured and orphaned wildlife, which are available in considerable variety. The objectives of Sorensen's program are to make it possible for inmates to contribute to the community and to acquire new skills. The program also has public educational value. In 1997, because her sponsors wanted an accounting of the program, Sorensen decided to evaluate it herself, initiating thus the project that was to become her master's thesis (Sorensen, 1998).

Neither her program nor the two in the United States had ever been scientifically studied or systematically evaluated. There is, however, a variety of studies on pet-facilitated therapy and animal-human bonding, although nearly all of these examine companion animals rather than wildlife. Touching companion animals is a major component of this kind of therapy and bonding, a practice that must be kept to a minimum, however, when dealing with animals from the wilds (to avoid habituation to humans, a maladaptive process when released to nature). In short, the state of the social science literature in the area of animal-human relations clearly justified an exploratory evaluation.

Sorensen interviewed with an interview guide a sample of 21 female and 39 male prison inmates who had participated in the program, in addition to a sample of five correctional officers and one manager working at the penal institution with which it is affiliated. In fact, except for a few who refused to be interviewed or who dropped out of the program, the 60 inmates constituted all who participated in it from February through August 1998. Sorensen randomly selected the five correctional officers, who together made up 39% of their group. All told, both samples, each being basically of the list variety, could be said to be sufficiently representative to allow generalization of the findings to all participants in and officers associated with the program.

The interviews with the inmates resulted in a number of observations. A large majority said they liked the program, mainly because it got them temporary release from prison, but with many adding that they liked it because it got them outdoors. Furthermore, many participants found the program appealing because they learned something and because it made them feel "human" and "normal" once again. The officers believed that it is the program that pulls the inmates to it rather than the prison pushing them toward it, but the officers were divided on whether it produces positive attitudes in the inmates. Nevertheless, the officers firmly believed that the program keeps inmates working and out of trouble within the prison. They also saw it as a way to build confidence and self-worth and increase prisoner happiness.

Sorensen makes several recommendations, one being that, where possible, inmates should be placed in community service programs that promote skill development, teamwork, communication, responsibility, and confidence building. Furthermore, inmates should be carefully matched to these programs, including those dealing with wildlife rehabilitation. Finally, she recommends that inmates become more involved than they are at present in training each other and in supervising workers at the facility. They should also be encouraged to make suggestions on facility operations. Transfer skills must also be taught, because once out of prison, it is difficult to find work in wildlife rehabilitation. For her sponsors, whether present or future,

Sorensen's thesis is serving as both an evaluation and an accounting of the program.

Conclusiveness and Generalizability

Because Sorensen's study was an evaluation, unlike the others presented in this chapter, it highlights somewhat more sharply than the rest a main limitation of exploration, namely, that this methodological approach fails to produce conclusive results. Exploratory findings are always hypothetical, and in her project, it was therefore impossible to conclude with certainty that the wildlife rehabilitation program plays a significant role in preventing recidivism among its former participants. Even her observation that a large majority of the participants liked the program, learned something while in it, and came away feeling human and normal once again are hypothetical, subject to controlled testing before they can be stamped as verified generalizations. In the sphere of evaluation, this uncertainty is especially unsettling. Unlike research scientists, who can wait for concatenation to unfold and conclusiveness to build as they go along, people with programs to be evaluated want quick answers, and they normally want stronger proof than hypotheses can give that all is going according to plan or, if it is not, that the faults identified are real and not merely hypothetical.

This is one point where skeptics might complain that exploration requires too much work for too little return: results that are inconclusive and ungeneralizable. And no doubt, some have eschewed exploration, in part, for this reason. Still, skeptics should note that inconclusiveness actually comes in degrees; research can be more or less inconclusive. The degree of inconclusiveness in exploratory research is reduced when the sample is *highly representative* and *tentative generalizability* is possible. Moreover, these two go together. Because both Harrison and Sorensen interviewed highly representative samples, they could say with a moderate degree of confidence that similar findings will be obtained in similar research settings located elsewhere. Compared with the studies of Smith, Sethi, and Hathaway, those of these two authors allow them to argue with greater assurance that, tentatively speaking, other researchers will come up with similar observations about the experience of home care transition and the effect of wildlife rehabilitation programs in, say, other North American urban health care and criminal corrections systems.

Tentative generalizability from exploration, although not absolutely conclusive, is far more conclusive and therefore more scientifically useful than at least three other ways of generating new ideas on the same phenomenon, notably, through pure speculation (done from the armchair with no empirical cases), serendipity, and unsystematic discovery research (e.g., using a small number of scattered empirical cases). In exploration, researchers make a concerted and systematic effort to understand through direct empirical observation a group, process, or activity. Even if sample representativeness is relatively weak, generalizations resulting from this effort have a significantly greater chance of being valid and generalizable than those resulting from pure speculation and similar approaches. Inconclusiveness and weak generalizability, although genuine limitations of exploration, are still not valid reasons for renouncing exploration as a major phase of the scientific process. They do suggest, however, that social science explorers must be both modest and candid in their claims about what a given exploratory study can and cannot accomplish in the way of generalizability and conclusiveness. Of course, to the extent that these scientists concatenate, they can become ever bolder in their assertions on such questions.

4. WRITING UP EXPLORATORY RESEARCH

Many social scientists, it appears, view with disdain the requirement that they write up the results of their research as a scholarly book, chapter, or journal article. This attitude toward one of the key norms of science—that research results be communicated—stems in part, I suspect, from the fact that writing social science is not commonly part of the training they received as graduate students. In addition, no time during that period of their lives did they, in the typical case, come to discover the joy of writing as a deeply satisfying and scientifically valuable activity in its own right. Under these conditions, writing, like correcting examinations, tends to be regarded as a necessary evil, the mandatory final leg of any particular research project, to be accomplished with dispatch so the author can get on with what he or she sees as more interesting work.

Writers of social science motivated thus are hardly likely to produce the scientific equivalent of *belles lettres*. Nor, happily, are they required to do so in most instances, because much of the time they are reporting technical material that would be difficult to convey in other than mechanical form. Work at the confirmatory level is normally highly quantitative, where writers have recourse to words only when they are unable to express their findings with graphs, charts, models, tables of figures, and similar devices.

It is different, however, when writing up exploratory research. Most of what is to be reported is not amenable to communication in quantitative form. Moreover, a main requirement in this approach is to write imaginatively and interestingly, even employing from time to time some of the conventions of creative writing. To be sure, the writer of exploratory research is neither a novelist nor a poet; he or she is first and foremost a scientist, and a theoretical one at that. But such literary devices as metaphor, story line, recurrent theme, and use of vivid description can enhance understanding of findings, generate rich theory, and make written text ever more appealing to both the scientific community and the general public, especially the small part that was under scrutiny.

Notwithstanding these remarks, this chapter is not so much about how to write up exploratory research in the sense just discussed. Fine treatments of this process already exist (e.g., Becker, 1986; Glaser, 1978, Chapter 8; Van Maanen, 1988; Wolcott, 1990), and I can add little to what these scholars have said. Instead, I address myself to certain problematic areas of writing in this field, areas that I have learned from experience with colleagues and students can cause considerable anxiety and lead to trouble during evaluation, whether as examination of a thesis submitted for a graduate degree or as appraisal of a manuscript submitted for possible publication. One such area is the corpus of literature that is seen to be related in some way to the explored group, process, or activity and the manner in which these received theories and findings are reviewed and incorporated in written exploratory text.

The Literature Review

The requirement that a literature review be undertaken prior to conducting a social science research project is one of the shibboleths of modern times. To be sure, exhaustive literature reviews are wholly justified as background for writing textbooks and review articles and for empirical or theoretical examinations of particular areas of research to determine the nature and scope of prior scientific activity there, so that proposed work will truly add to the corpus of writings. Problems emerge, however, when this approach is applied without modification, as it often is by researchers who are largely unfamiliar with exploration, to projects designed to discover new ideas.

By contrast, literature reviews in exploratory research are carried out to demonstrate that little or no work has been done on the group, process, or activity under consideration and that an open-ended approach to data collection is, therefore, wholly justified. The procedure I have followed over the years is first to search for the study or studies that come closest to examining what I want to examine and then to show how these studies leave unexplored certain critical aspects of that phenomenon. In the literature review, I devote the greatest amount of space to these works, after which, proceeding as if by concentric rings, I devote less and less space to works increasingly removed from my project.

Accordingly, compared with literature reviews in confirmatory research, those in true exploratory research are necessarily short. This brevity, as might be suspected, often alarms social scientists unacquainted with the conventions of exploration. But the pressure to review past work in the way this is done at the confirmatory level must be resisted, for to stuff the research report with an extensive tour of marginally related studies makes for heavy and distracting reading. This practice diminishes considerably a work's literary quality, which, as just noted, is especially important in this phase of the scientific process.

This is not to argue, however, that marginally related studies should be ignored everywhere in research reports containing exploratory data. True, in the main or formal literature review, which conventionally appears as a special, usually early section of the written text, the content should focus on the most closely related studies. But exploratory researchers, when presenting their findings in later sections of the report, do nevertheless refer occasionally to some of the more remotely related studies, thereby showing how their own findings support or contradict them. These links give exploratory data some additional intellectual anchorage; they show how the data relate to the wider scholarly world. Moreover, it is always important to note where existing ideas are supported or contradicted by new data. And challenging received theory and research demonstrates further the important role that discovery research plays in circumventing the logical constraints of syllogistic reasoning.

Supremacy of Generalizations

Another reason why unnecessarily long literature reviews are to be avoided in exploratory research is that they tend, because of their length, to hog some of the limelight in the report. But the limelight in this genre of social science writing belongs exclusively to the generalizations that have emerged from open-ended data. Because they are the study's raison d'être, nothing, literature reviews included, should be allowed to upstage them. Furthermore, the principle of supremacy of generalizations should also guide the structuring of the report. That is, they should be clearly stated, perhaps at the beginning of a paragraph or section or as a sort of list in a summary or conclusions. With some authors, however, the open-ended nature of exploratory research carries over into their writing, it too becoming fluid and wandering. Although there are times when this quality may be desirable, too much of it can lead to loss of a sense of purpose and direction in the report, with the emergent generalizations being the first to disappear from view.

One problem frequently faced by writers of exploratory research is the need to qualify, often extensively, their generalizations. For example, I observed that husbands commonly oppose any involvement in barbershop singing by their wives that amounts to more than routine rehearsing and performing in the hobby (Stebbins, 1996, pp. 77-78). Husbands tend to express their disapproval when wives take up an administrative activity or leave town to attend a weekend workshop. Still, there were important exceptions to discuss, such as the husbands who encourage this sort of thing and the meanings that both husbands and wives attach to these additional involvements. In all this, I gradually became aware that I was losing track of the principal generalization that anchored this part of the report, with the result that I had to rewrite certain paragraphs in that section. In fact, generalizations are rarely simple and straightforward; they must usually be qualified, put in context, and related to other generalizations. The challenge is to keep them from becoming submerged in the ensuing discussion.

Quoting Respondents

But nothing seems to more quickly upstage a generalization than a long-winded quotation from a respondent or a string of shorter ones from several respondents. I am not sure why this is so. Perhaps it is the momentary relief for readers that they find appealing when the text changes from relatively heavy theory building (presenting, qualifying, and interrelating generalizations) to lighter, more ordinary fare. In the latter case, readers enter directly the realm of human interest where the reading is easy. Interestingly, although journalists have used this device, possibly since the invention of newspapers, their work is instructive with respect to the principle of supremacy of generalizations, for it is often impossible to find any in standard, idiographic journalistic accounts of current events.

Such journalistic tendencies should be minimized, and the best exploratory researchers manage to do this in their writing, not only because they want to stay with their mission of developing grounded theory, but also because they want to keep their generalizations at center stage. Glaser (1978) counseled, "The most important thing to remember is to *write about concepts not people.* [italics in original] . . . The power of theory resides in concepts, not description" (p. 134). Because respondent quotations are but one form of description, when they are available, I try to adhere to the rule of, on average, adding a substantial one about every second manuscript page (double-spaced). I am aware that these passages neither prove nor validate my generalizations; they only illustrate them. Proof, to the extent it is possible in exploration, and validity rest on the number of times a regularity of thought or behavior is observed in talk or action, which must be often enough to seem general to all or to a main segment of the people in the group, process, or activity being examined. To be sure, particular statements made by respondents in interviews are the raw materials investigators work with to fashion their generalizations, but subsequently quoting in the report some of these statements can never show, validate, or prove the creative leaps the investigator makes during these expressions of intellectual craftsmanship.

Nevertheless, this advice needs some tempering, when it comes to personality-centered research. In it, the personalities studied as cases or presented through narratives must also be placed in the limelight. Here, the author must coordinate respondent quotations, descriptive case material, and exploratory generalizations such that none overshadows the others, a neat but still possible turn of writing prowess. Much the same can be said for language-centered research, where precisely recorded utterances made by respondents are quoted verbatim in the research report as the first step toward generalizing about them.

If interviewee testimonials play only an illustrative role in community-centered exploratory research, it follows that exact quotations of them are by no means always necessary in such work. Because, most of the time, the respondents quoted are not personally identified, verbatim accuracy is, in reality, unimportant. As long as it illustrates the generalization and conveys what the respondent meant to say, the quotation can, in fact, be a paraphrase of his or her original statement. Many a graduate student could save countless hours of transcription time and many a professional researcher could avoid huge transcription expenses if only they would accept this principle. Why go through the time-consuming process of word-for-word transcription of an entire exploratory interview when such precision is unnecessary? Of course, even if researchers only intend to paraphrase their respondents' observations, they must still thoroughly assess each interview, reviewing carefully the accompanying fieldnotes and audiotapes. And some transcription may be desirable for this purpose.

Whichever is used in a research report, paraphrasing or verbatim quotation (and one might use both at different points in the text), the writer should be clear about what he or she is doing. In other words, never use quotation marks with paraphrases, and if a paraphrased passage is set off as a block, inform the reader that it is not a direct quote or write that, "in effect," Respondent X said the following.

On the Nature of Generalizations

Considered in this section are two issues concerning exploratory generalizations that I have yet to see treated in the methodological literature on qualitative research in the social sciences. One centers on the use of quantitative terms in these propositions. The other deals with the grammatical tense in which they are presented.

In this book, a *quantitative generalization* is defined as an empirical observation expressed in numerical form. For instance, I once wrote in an article on amateur astronomers that more than 80% of the sample find personal enrichment and self-development to be rewarding features of their avocation and that more than 50% of them see its self-expressive aspects in the same light (Stebbins, 1981, p. 293). This article, written at a time when and in a discipline where exploration was even less well understood than at present, contained many quantitative generalizations of this kind, an accommodation to editorial pressure that I would have resisted today.

Why is the quantitative generalization to be avoided in writing up exploratory research? First, such generalizations are, in fact, quite misleading, because with the frequent addition and deletion of questions in the interview guide (as part of theoretical sampling), the base number used to compute the proportions can fluctuate widely, depending on the question under consideration. Second, using figures such as 50% and 80% suggests a degree of precision seldom seen in exploration. I could have written that "about half" or a "substantial majority" of the respondents did or said something and as effectively conveyed my observations as if I had reported them quantitatively. Third, the goal of exploratory research is to generate grounded theory and the hypotheses that compose it. Exploration rarely, if ever, leads to predictions as precise as numerical proportions. Rather, it leads to vaguer predictions such as a majority of respondents find as rewarding the personal enrichment and self-development features of their avocation. Let precision, then, be added in the confirmatory phase, where appropriate research designs, sampling techniques, and measuring instruments are available for this. With a decent base of exploration from which to work, confirmatory studies may well be able to demonstrate some day, within a reasonable margin of error, that in their avocation, 80% of amateur astronomers do realize these two rewards.

Turning to the issue of grammatical tense, it might come as a surprise to some that, given widespread preference for the past tense in reporting scientific data, the most efficient way of reporting exploratory generalizations is, nonetheless, to use instead the present tense. The propositions about astronomers and barbershop singers presented earlier in this chapter were written in the present tense, which is, of course, the usual tense of hypotheses when set out in reports of confirmatory research. My advice to writers of exploratory research, then, is to ignore the tradition in confirmatory research of presenting research results in the past tense. Rather, I suggest that they present their results in the present tense, in harmony with the practice in verification of presenting hypotheses in that tense. After all, the goal of exploratory research reports is to present a set of hypotheses knitted together as grounded theory, with the entire ensemble to be confirmed later. In addition, the generalizations of exploratory research often bear on continuing groups, processes, and activities that in no way cease with completion of the study. These propositions or hypotheses are not so much findings of an investigation conducted in the past as statements about a social world functioning in the present, perhaps even the future, depending on the degree of stability of the phenomena observed.

The scientific world would not end were explorers to continue, by habit and identification with confirmatory research, to write up their observations in the past tense, even if exploration would be denied a minor efficiency should the practice continue. And although such terms as *findings* and *results* are not really tense bound, they are general to all types of research, unlike such terms as *observation* and *generalization,* which are more exclusively associated with exploration and thus more effectively communicate the aura of discovery. I have tried in this book to privilege the second set, even though literary style has sometimes forced me to rely on the first as well.

Validity and Reliability

Another reigning shibboleth, equal in stature to that of the literature review, is the requirement that validity and reliability be assured in all social science research, the exploratory variety included. These two conditions bear on the design and conduct of such research and must, in any report of it, be addressed to the satisfaction of critical readers and the canons of the discipline. Indeed, it is important that, in the report, an explorer present his or her observations in a manner that assures readers that these two concerns have been properly dealt with.

The question of validity in exploratory research, which goes at times by the name of *credibility,* refers to whether a researcher can gain an accurate or true impression of the group, process, or activity under study and, if so, how this can be accomplished. Validity is problematic in this realm of social scientific inquiry in at least three ways:

1. Reactive effects of the observer's presence or activities on the phenomenon being observed
2. Distorting effects of selective perception and interpretation on the observer's part
3. Limitations on the observer's ability to witness all relevant aspects of the phenomena in question. (McCall & Simmons, 1969, p. 78)

These three problems worry exploratory and confirmatory researchers alike, although the latter seem more concerned about them than the former. Viewed from the angle of confirmatory research, exploration appears to evoke the greatest suspicion with reference to the second problem, primarily because of the heavy subjective element involved when a lone researcher (the usual way exploration is conducted) observes and interviews, employing an open-ended design.

Exploratory researchers try to enhance the validity of their studies in various ways. For one, many of them discuss their emergent generalizations with the people they are investigating to determine if these ideas have a familiar ring, that in the eyes of these people, the generalizations seem plausible. Some participants in investigations may even be given written text to read. In addition, aware that personal bias can distort perception and interpretation of observed events, competent explorers look assiduously for evidence that might contradict their observations. This approach is successful to the extent that the researcher is aware of his or her biases—and it is likely that no one is fully aware of them all—and that they are not held with great, unbending conviction. Third, these researchers constantly ask themselves whether they have observed a sufficient number of occurrences of an event, process, or activity to constitute grounds for a valid generalization.

Often overlooked in discussions about validity in exploratory research is the fact that the most effective way to ensure it, and in that fashion solve the three problems, is to concatenate research projects in the area of study. Separate studies by different scholars centered on the same or related groups, processes, or activities will, over time, result in the most solid and convincing validations possible of the concepts and generalizations emerging from this body of research. In other words, a scientific field, like the city of Rome, is (was) not built in a day. When social scientists are putting the finishing touches on an area of research—polishing measuring instruments, testing critical differences in generalizations, mapping distributions of the phenomenon being investigated—it is reasonable to worry about the validity of each study. Potentially, each could be the definitive work that yields the best possible instrument, tests most effectively the differences in question, or maps with greatest precision the distribution of certain ideas or behaviors.

Exploration lacks this sense of finality. Rather, many studies must be undertaken to generate a convincingly valid, wide-ranging grounded theory. Hence, little is gained by insisting that any one of them be regarded as the final link in the exploratory-confirmatory chain. Exploratory researchers should concern themselves with validity—about that, there should be no doubt—and they should do so particularly with reference to the three problems identified by McCall and Simmons (1969). They should do their best to ensure it, recognizing, however, that their efforts in this regard for any single study will be only partially successful and that they will have to wait for future explorations before the tale of validity is fully told.

Reliability refers to the replicability of a researcher's observations; it turns on the question of whether another researcher with similar methodological training, understanding of the field setting, and rapport with its subjects can make similar observations. The same three problems identified earlier by McCall and Simmons (1969) also affect reliability in exploratory research. Here, too, after all the fretting about reliability in a particular study, experience remains the best teacher: Sufficient concatenation with different researchers participating in the process is needed to demonstrate most convincingly that they can make similar or compatible observations on the same or related groups, processes, or activities. Moreover, as with validity, great concern with reliability of the study at hand is most appropriate toward the end of the research chain, where confirmation is the rule, compared with the beginning of that chain, where exploration dominates. More extensive treatments of validity and reliability in qualitative research are available from Kirk and Miller (1986) and Stewart (1998).

50

Conclusions

The foregoing discussion, devoted as it was to how to solve certain problems in writing exploratory social science, failed to cover one key point. Such writing is more than communication of observations, as important as this happens to be; it is also a creative process, wherein new scientific ideas are born. These new ideas spring from juxtaposing in drafts of written text emergent generalizations from the group, process, or activity under examination. The logics of the language and the argument being used facilitate this process. John Steinbeck, although he never attributed this kind of creativity directly to writing, observed more generally that "new ideas are like rabbits. You get a couple and learn how to handle them and pretty soon you have a dozen." More rabbits come into this world, as it were, when words, phrases, ideas, and data bump against each other during the production of written text. If social scientists never wrote prose, preferring to communicate their ideas only orally or quantitatively, many fewer new ideas would become available on the intellectual marketplace. Put otherwise, failing to write stunts the growth of grounded theory, perhaps even all types of theory.

But there is an Achilles' heel of exploration that was exposed in the preceding exposition about how to achieve optimum validity and reliability in this approach. What if individual researchers and the research community in general fail, as the practice has largely been, to concatenate the new field of discovery? What, then, of the validity and reliability of the sole study undertaken there? The answer is obvious: A sole study will be seriously weaker than if there were more studies. The cure for this weakness lies in successfully persuading more social science researchers to commit themselves to discovery research and adopt the lifestyle of exploration, where concatenation becomes an integral part of their professional way of life.

5. THE EXPLORER

If social scientists have tended to overlook exploration as process and methodological approach, they have established an even worse record of avoidance when it comes to considering the explorers themselves, people for whom discovery is a pervasive personal orientation, an occupation, or, as this chapter suggests, a vocation. Such an omission is critical, for obviously, somebody must explore, if exploratory data are to be gathered and tentative hypotheses formed, and, as obviously, the social sciences need knowledge about the type of person who has a talent and passion for discovery, if they are to encourage scholars in this line of work. What, then, in concrete terms, is an explorer? What sort of life does he or she live? What motivates some researchers to explore only once or twice and others to make a career of this genre of inquiry?

The focus of this chapter, however, is not on the more or less full-time field-worker, a figure who epitomizes the work of anthropology, where field-workers are immersed in the everyday life of, for instance, an urban group, rural community, or peasant or primitive society. The lifestyle of this type of researcher has already been richly analyzed by Rose (1990). Rather, attention is restricted here to the more common social science practice of part-time involvement, as carried out in participant observation, semistructured interviewing, and analyses of written and oral texts. Researchers of the latter bent, when not in the field, normally return to their homes or their offices (or perhaps hotel rooms), base points for the pursuit of other familial and occupational obligations.

What Is an Explorer?

Social science explorers are, first and foremost, theorists. This assertion may come as a surprise to some readers, given that explorers are so directly and intensely involved in data collection and given the considerable amount of attention devoted in this book to this aspect of discovery. Nevertheless, in taking the broad view, the avowed perspective here, I want to stress again that theory is the primary goal of exploratory research, that grounded data are only a means to this end, and that therefore explorers are, in the final analysis, theorists, albeit highly empirical ones compared with their speculative cousins, who prefer their armchairs to fieldwork.

It is necessary to underscore the fact that explorers are theorists, because reigning images of theorists and researchers in the social sciences exclude them. Most social scientists, if asked, I believe would describe as a theorist someone who generates theory either by pure speculation or by logico-deductive synthesis of existing studies and theoretical arguments. Because exploration is foreign to most of them, these scholars would not typically include as a kind of theoretical undertaking inductive generation of propositions from directly gathered data. On the other side of the coin, researchers are commonly seen as people who do verification work framed by the established theories and ideas of a particular field of study and who collect data there for testing certain hypotheses or describing certain phenomena. As pointed out earlier, emphasis here is on, among other things, techniques of data collection and validity and reliability of the data gathered. Theory, although hardly irrelevant in this sphere of social science, is nonetheless a decidedly more distant concern. It is normally left to theorists, as just described, to do the real theoretical work in the area, which they rarely do in reports of empirical research but rather do in separate treatises written expressly for this purpose.

The explorer-theorist is, in short, an *inductive theorist,* a label that distinguishes this type of social scientist from *deductive theorists,* whose role was described in the preceding paragraph. These labels are important, in this instance, especially for exploratory researchers who, as will become evident shortly, get caught up in the day-to-day details of gathering data and, later, in the equally absorbing process of writing them into a report. In the heat of these battles, they all too frequently forget their principal mission: the generation of theory (descriptive concepts, generic concepts, generalizations). It is hoped, then, that if they can come to view themselves primarily as inductive theorists, they will become more inclined to focus their data collection on areas of social life that lead to substantial generalizations and to write in ways, set out in the preceding chapter, that enhance their communication and elaboration of emerging grounded theory.

Lifestyle

C. Wright Mills (1959) understood very well the lifestyle of the social science explorer, even if, in his writings, he never identified this person as such:

> It is best to begin, I think, by reminding you, the beginning student, that the most admirable thinkers within the scholarly community you have chosen to join do not split their work from their lives. They seem to take both too seriously to allow such dissociation, and they want to use each for the enrichment of the other. . . . Scholarship is a choice of how to live as well as a choice of career. . . .
>
> What this means is that you must learn to use your life experience in your intellectual work: continually to examine and interpret it. . . . To say that you can "have experience," means, for one thing, that your past plays into and affects your present and that it defines your capacity for future experience. As a social scientist, you have to control this rather elaborate interplay to capture what you experience and sort it out. (pp. 195-196)

In effect, Mills envisioned a research lifestyle in which the individual becomes immersed, turning many of his or her waking hours into the pursuit of original data that will foster understanding of the group, process, or activity being investigated.

He further advised researchers to establish a file in which they can store their thoughts, periodical clippings, scholarly references, and anything else that might possibly bear on their exploratory interests. Eight years later, Glaser and Strauss (1967, pp. 108, 112) echoed this idea in a somewhat more technical way when they described the process of memo writing, arguing forcefully for its importance in conducting grounded theory research. Common to these three authors is the observation that explorers in the social sciences are continually thinking about their research projects, doing this quite outside the field where they are actively observing, interviewing, and reading relevant archival material. New ideas can "pop up" literally at any time during a researcher's waking hours, while reading a newspaper, watching television, taking a walk, and enjoying many other occasions in everyday life. The contents of the file and the memos to oneself, whatever their provenance, constitute potentially precious insights, which later could well get converted into solid generalizations, which, in turn, will find a place in the emerging grounded theory.

Personal experience, then, is not to be ignored in exploration, nor, for that matter, is the relevant experience of others, be they friends, relatives, or participants in the group, process, or activity under study (Glaser & Strauss, 1967, pp. 252-253). Such experience constitutes one important component of what can be called the *analytic lifestyle* of exploratory research. A second important component, which makes this lifestyle still more absorbing, is the tendency for researchers to want to contemplate what has been observed in their research projects during times of the day when they are not in the field. It is as if explorers, caught up in the novelty of their observations, are unable to put them completely aside when enacting other roles in their lives, as in enjoying leisure, parenting, or carrying out domestic chores. Finding new ideas through personal experience and spontaneous analysis makes up a highly absorbing part of the exploratory researcher's analytic lifestyle.

Furthermore, social scientists of this bent also lead a *practical lifestyle*. Particularly those who collect data by means of participant observation find that, while in the field, they must conform to someone else's schedule and mode of living. My study of stand-up comics (Stebbins, 1990) exemplifies this situation well. It required that, for several months, I attend at least a couple of nightclub shows a week, with new comics arriving at the beginning of every week most times of the year. Because the nature of audiences varies according to time of evening, I had to observe both first and second shows, with the latter typically ending between midnight and 1 a.m. Following the shows, I sometimes benefitted from "hanging out" after hours with the comics, in that I gained a feeling for that facet of their lifestyle. Interviews took place by and large during afternoons or early evenings. Moreover, because the study was Canada-wide, many sessions of observation and interviewing took place in cities outside Calgary, my home. All this was carried out in addition to full-time teaching, and while I was collecting data, this resulted in a vastly reduced family and leisure life. For me, a person who likes to be in bed by 10:30 p.m. and to rise at about 6 a.m., the study of comics brought a truly different daily routine.

In all this, the researcher is apt to be alone, in that team research is uncommon in exploration. It is not that team research is to be avoided, because it often makes good sense to explore with a colleague or two who can bring special qualifications to the project and whose interest in it is at least as profound as that of the principal researcher. Still, as normally happens, social science explorers get committed to projects of interest only to them and so must pursue those projects on their own until their accumulated work on the group, process, or activity that is their passion attracts some followers. Because they must necessarily work outside conventional spheres of theory and research in their disciplines, exploratory researchers, at least during early phases of the exploratory process, are likely to be marginal people there. In this regard, I suspect it would even be possible to demonstrate that they are not usually members of the most venerated university departments in their disciplines.

Of course, lone explorers are only alone with respect to professional company. If their research is going well and requires direct human contact, they are normally heavily involved with people in the field. In fact, this side of the practical lifestyle puts a premium on interpersonal relations skills. For here, the researcher must be able to get along with strangers, know how to respond as a guest in their world to problems that emerge while he or she is there, and do these things while maintaining his or her role as a social scientist. Not easy, particularly because the social sciences in general and exploratory research in particular are not widely understood by the general public. In many of my studies, no small number of respondents thought I was conducting research for a graduate thesis, an impression that persisted even after I explained in a letter the purpose of my research and the reasons for undertaking it. Moreover, some were surprised to learn that I had no hypotheses to test but intended instead to generate them. In this regard, a school board in St. John's, Newfoundland, once refused to grant permission for me to study the ways teachers working under its jurisdiction define certain classroom situations, a rejection based entirely on the fact (so I was told) that its members saw exploration as scientifically weak.

Motivation and Career

How does a person become committed to a research problem that is best studied through exploration? To my knowledge, no one has ever examined this question, even though the results of such inquiry would surely provide useful information on how to encourage more social scientists to adopt this approach. From digging into my own research past and the experience of my students and colleagues who have done exploratory work, as well as perusing some of the biographies written by social science explorers (e.g., Mead, 1972; Mills, 1959; Reinharz, 1979), I can nevertheless offer some suggestions. One is that would-be explorers embark on a research career that enables them to delve into one or more of their own central life interests. According to Robert Dubin (1992), a central life interest is "that portion of a person's total life in which energies are invested in both physical/ intellectual activities and in positive emotional states" (p. 41). Sociologically, a central life interest is often associated with a major work, leisure, or domestic role. True, some of these interests may have already been scientifically examined, possibly leaving little scope for further exploration. Yet even in this situation, the suggestion still holds, although the person with such an interest will find a career mainly in verification research.

But to repeat an earlier observation, innumerable areas of social life remain largely, if not entirely, unexplored. The field of leisure, for example, is full of unexplored groups, processes, and activities, and it is by no means the only area of life where would-be explorers might have strong interests. Others include religion, politics, education, family life, and interpersonal relations, to mention a few. Many a social scientist has, in fact, followed the irresistible call to research given off by a central life interest. The result has been a social science enriched over the years with knowledge about such phenomena as housework, taxi driving, and prison life, as well as running for and holding political office. When I entered sociology in the early 1960s, I joined a handful of colleagues who, like me, were both enthusiastic jazz musicians and committed social scientists eager to scientifically explore their art and its practitioners as part of their scholarly careers. Gail Perry (2000), a new Christian, became fascinated with the mechanisms by which greater faith enhances well-being, a relationship found in established theory but one that had never been explored for its everyday life implications.

It is also true that social scientists occasionally get so enamored of theoretical questions or practical ones bearing on measurement that they become not only central life interests in their own right but also springboards from which to launch a substantial career in one of the social sciences, usually in hypothesis-based research or logico-deductive theory construction. Yet it happens as often, I believe, that occupational specialities of this sort fail to become central in Dubin's (1992) sense of the word. Social scientists in this situation soon lose interest in their scholarly careers, leading many to contravene the publishing norms of their university and, as an adaptation to this predicament, to seek an alternative career in administration or teaching or to opt out completely by taking early retirement. Had these souls found a research career centered on one of their nonwork central life interests, perhaps this story would have had a different and, for them, happier ending.

The concatenation of exploratory studies is another key to finding a career in discovery research. Certainly, the myriad research possibilities that become evident on completion of the first exploration, when considered together, add up to a strong temptation to push ahead with another project that will further expand and elaborate the nascent grounded theory. The explorer's sense of the importance of his or her present and future work in understanding the explored group, process, or activity and the importance assigned to it by colleagues in their assessment can also whet the appetite for concatenation. But such a career will die aborning if no real commitment to this progression develops. For their commitment to take root, explorers must recognize that the advantages of concatenation outweigh significantly its disadvantages. With the former having been set out in Chapter 1, it remains only to examine the latter.

Possibly the most preeminent disadvantage of concatenated exploration is that it is always tiring and in some way uncomfortable. Social scientists typically wind up their careers in field research after one or two studies, often because field exploration makes heavy demands on their time, upsets their daily routines, and can, in some projects, put them in touch with people who are disagreeably different from them, perhaps increasingly so as the researcher grows older and, like other aging people, develops an ever more individuated personality (Berno, Moore, & Raymore, 1998, pp. 300-301). Long-term concatenation extends indefinitely the disagreeable aspects of this kind of scholarly work.

Furthermore, the unpleasant side of fieldwork, sometimes combined with other forces, can make researchers jaded. This disadvantage attenuates exploration of groups, activities, and social processes, because it dulls sensitivity to the unique aspects of each new research setting; in other words, it reduces a person's capacity for discovery. Moreover, evolving grounded theory can have a similar effect, channeling researcher insight too closely, too strictly along the lines of its propositions. And, on top of this, a sense of déjà vu can set in as the years and projects go by. If not actively opposed, these diverse conditions can become formidable barriers to the generation of new observations unless, of course, theoretical saturation has been reached and it is time to turn to verification concerns.

Last, as indicated in earlier discussions of the methodological and theoretical foundations of exploration, concatenation sooner or later pushes researchers toward the second column of Figure 1. Comparisons within the set of studies make this progression inevitable; it unfolds as the researcher develops increasingly broader generalizations to account for similarities and differences, with the generalizations then being interwoven on an ever more abstract plane. Now, column 2 is a true theoretical and methodological limbo, for both the exploratory and the confirmatory models of research are, as noted previously, essentially polar ideal types. What is more, even though the vast majority of research projects in contemporary social science seem only to approach these types, they are nevertheless judged with reference to them.

It follows that book and journal article manuscripts falling between the two types could suffer exceptionally high rates of rejection, to the extent that editors and reviewers are guided exclusively by one or the other. The alternative, which appears to be uncommon, is that authors of texts reporting concatenated explorations would be asked to modify them to fit more closely one ideal typical model or the other. In either situation, exploratory researchers who assemble over many years a lengthy chain of studies will at this point likely encounter among no small number of their colleagues an annoying lack of understanding of the methodological and theoretical foundations of column 2. Specifically, it will be difficult for them to find gatekeepers in the publishing world who recognize that the middle of Figure 1 is a legitimate stage in the development of knowledge in the social sciences, perhaps even an ideal-typical model of research and theory of its own.

Yet this disadvantage can also be interpreted as a cardinal strength of concatenated exploration, for it makes available to qualitative researchers the opportunity to push the study of sets of related groups, processes, or activities toward increased methodological and theoretical rigor (both qualitative and quantitative) as development of their grounded theories allows. As on-site overseers of the larger project, so to speak, they are unlikely to jump to premature theoretical closure or methodological sophistication, in the sense that they would terminate exploration when it was still needed. Meanwhile, outsiders to the chain of studies in question are unlikely to have this insight and, lacking it, to commit precisely this error.

Conclusions

Need for a systematic, long-term approach to qualitative exploration has never been more acute, given the contemporary growth in popularity of qualitative research with its considerable accumulation of one-shot, open-ended field studies. The advantages, in outweighing the disadvantages, support this conviction. Moreover, as the late Carl Couch (1991) concluded, "The failure of many qualitative researchers to observe and analyze social processes and relationships and to employ comparative procedures has lessened the contributions they could make to sociological lore" (p. 161). Scholarly careers in concatenated exploration constitute an important remedy for this deficiency, an idea whose time has clearly come.

Opting for a career in social science exploration is also a timely choice in another important way: Widespread social change, already the hall-mark of modern life, is destined to grow in the future. How will society and the social sciences deal with the multitude of transformations soon to face the world when the discovery of new ideas is constrained by syllogistic reasoning?

6. EXPLORATION: ITS FUTURE IN THE SOCIAL SCIENCES

The chapters in this book demonstrate that the social science explorer has, in reality, three faces: methodologist, writer, and theorist. Other social scientists, of course, have something to do with methodology, writing, and theory, too, expressed in the ways they go about gathering their data, analyzing them, and writing them up. But as argued here for confirmatory research, emphasis on these three is unequal, with most of it being placed on methodology. By contrast, the exploratory researcher gives strong weighting to all three, although my view has been throughout that, if forced to present one face only, he or she must present that of theorist, in particular that of inductive theorist (see Chapter 5). If for no other reason than it is the least understood and recognized face in all of social science, this is an affirmation that I have been saying holds all too well even in qualitative research circles.

Explorers in the social sciences, it may be concluded, are more likely to be renaissance people than their counterparts working the confirmatory mainstream of these disciplines. Explorers must be equally proficient at designing and conducting research (only their kind, to be sure), writing about it, and generating theory, whereas people who do not explore can specialize by becoming theorists or statistical experts or by pursuing an interest in testing hypotheses in a highly specialized area. Nonetheless, the broad-based explorer who hunts high and low for new data and ideas capable of shedding light on the group, process, activity, or situation under study has an important role to play in the Information Age, in the electronically dominated world in which most of humankind now lives. This claim holds despite the seemingly better fit in this world of the confirmatory specialist, whose logico-deductive procedures are in perfect or nearly perfect harmony with the workings of the computer.

Exploration in the Information Age

Exploration is an important approach for social research in the Information Age, not in the least because this age generates rapid and widespread change. Manuel Castells (1996) has observed that "a technological revolution, centered around information technologies, is reshaping, at accelerated pace, the material basis of society," and a few paragraphs later, he writes that, in the modern world, "social changes are as dramatic as technological and economic processes of transformation" (pp. 1-2). Castells describes in considerable detail these social, economic, and technological changes, obviating the need to repeat here his many observations. To get an idea of the scope of change now afoot, one need only consider just some of the effects flowing from the invention of the cellular telephone:

- It is a new way to communicate with the outside world while walking or driving a vehicle.
- Its existence has led to new laws to control "cell phone" use while behind the wheel.
- It is a new way to report emergencies and foil criminal intent.
- It provides new opportunities for investment in and manufacture of the telephones themselves as well as advertising about and sales of these instruments.

Of importance for the purposes of this book are the twin facts that diverse changes of this sort and their ever ramifying effects will require extensive scientific examination, and exploration will, in the large majority of instances, be the most fruitful approach by which to accomplish this. Moreover, to avoid conducting just another "cute" isolated study, discovery work on new phenomena of the day, including cell phones, will have to be integrated into the relevant literature in the manner described in Chapter 4, giving new studies additional intellectual anchorage by showing how the data relate to the wider scholarly world. Thus, by way of example, findings on cell phone use could well have implications for the ways certain organizations function, families and friends stay in touch with each other, and predatory criminals select their victims. In short, discovery through exploration is explanation, which is made possible both by generating grounded theory about the new group, process, and so on and by situating that theory in the context of the larger society.

The limitations of syllogistic reasoning indicate that, under conditions of rapid and widespread change, more than ever in modern history, many important groups, processes, activities, and situations will remain hidden well beyond the line of sight of most social scientists. And their neglect will continue unless someone seizes the opportunity to explore these areas. Furthermore, in this sphere of inquiry, the computer will be of little help. Aronowitz and DiFazio (1994), in writing about the place of the computer and the Information Age in education, hold that

> The computer is not designed to anticipate or respond to problems that lie outside its logical ordering. So the computer may be used to uncover the epistemological foundations of technological thinking that is rule-driven rather than context-driven, but it cannot be taken as a model for thought. It is an *interested* [italics in original] machine beautifully designed for some purposes and not for others. (p. 133)

Speaking figuratively, they note that context-driven thinking occurs "where knowledge of the terrain must be obtained more by intuition, memory, and specific knowledge of the actors or the geography than by mastering logical rules" (p. 133). The computer programs discussed earlier, which are designed to aid exploratory research, are likewise not instruments of discovery; they are no more than useful administrative tools for organizing data and ideas already found or generated.

If the need for exploration has never been greater, the lot of the social science explorer has not, for all that, grown any easier. For example, exploratory science, particularly at its creative, inventive core, seems highly resistant to significant technological assistance. For instance, audio- and videotape recorders are unquestionably handy devices in the field, and when researchers will be able to efficiently download their recordings into a computer, they will save a good deal of time while enhancing accuracy of their data. But all this only aids creativity; it in no way substitutes for it. With respect to its most central operations, then, exploration seems destined to remain a sort of scholarly cottage industry in an era when much of the rest of life will be far more intimately connected with, if not dependent on, the microchip.

So exploration will always be home for the intellectual adventurer, the academic Columbuses of the day, who suspect the existence of something outside conventional wisdom and thought that is worthy of systematic examination. For them, the cottage-industry character of exploration will matter little; indeed, it may well hold great appeal for that very reason. Nor is being marginalized in this way likely to deter their inclination toward discovery. The excitement of their research careers will carry them through, whatever the social and psychological problems encountered from working under these conditions.

Perhaps most unsettling for committed social science explorers is the current proclivity in government and industry for funding research that aims to solve practical problems and to dismiss as unimportant discovery research (Aronowitz & DiFazio, 1994, pp. 340-341). Generally speaking, exploration in the social sciences, compared with confirmation there, is not an expensive undertaking, but some financial assistance is still necessary, and sometimes, as in the need to use distant archives or live for many months in another country, the cost of research can mount significantly. This is one problem associated with being marginal that is neither easily solved nor casually dismissed.

I hope, then, that it is clear from what has been said in this book that exploration is by no means for everyone. But I hope, too, that it is equally clear by now that it must be for someone. There is a tremendous amount of sociocultural change afoot in today's world. To ignore it is both foolish and perilous. Let exploration, then, assume its rightful place in the world of the social sciences, and let those scholars there who would take it up find in their research lives what Einstein found in his.

The most beautiful thing we can experience is the Mysterious.
It is the source of all true art and science.
Einstein, What I believe, *Forum,* October 1930

62

REFERENCES

Adler, E. S., & Clark, R. (1999). *How it's done: An invitation to social research.* Belmont, CA: Wadsworth.

Altheide, D. L., & Johnson, J. M. (1994). Criteria for assessing interpretive validity in qualitative research. In N. K. Denzin & Y. S. Lincoln (Eds.), *Handbook of qualitative research* (pp. 485-499). Thousand Oaks, CA: Sage.

Aronowitz, S., & DiFazio, W. (1994). *The jobless future: Sci-tech and the dogma of work.* Minneapolis: University of Minnesota Press.

Ball, D. W. (1965). Sarcasm as sociation: The rhetoric of interaction. *Canadian Review of Sociology and Anthropology, 2,* 190-198.

Ball, D. W. (1968). Toward a sociology of telephones and telephoners. In M. Truzzi (Ed.), *Sociology and everyday life* (pp. 59-74). Englewood Cliffs, NJ: Prentice Hall.

Becker, H. S. (1986). *Writing for social scientists: How to start and finish your thesis, book, or article.* Chicago: University of Chicago Press.

Berno, T., Moore, K., & Raymore, L. (1998). The psychology of leisure, recreation, and tourism in New Zealand and the South Pacific. In H. C. Perkins & G. Cushman (Eds.), *Time out: Leisure, recreation, and tourism in New Zealand and Australia* (pp. 288-309). Auckland, NZ: Addison Wesley Longman New Zealand.

Blumer, H. (1969). *Symbolic interactionism.* Englewood Cliffs, NJ: Prentice Hall.

Boulding, K. (1958). Evidences for an administrative science: A preview of the *Administrative Science Quarterly,* volumes 1 and 2. *Administrative Science Quarterly, 3,* 1-21.

Castells, M. (1996). *The information age: Economy, society, and culture: Vol. 1. The rise of the network society.* Oxford, UK: Blackwell.

Clanton, G., & Smith, L. G. (1977). *Jealousy.* Englewood Cliffs, NJ: Prentice Hall.

Couch, C. J. (1984). Symbolic interaction and generic sociological principles. *Symbolic Interaction, 7,* 1-14.

Couch, C. J. (1991). Review of *The dilemma of qualitative research: Herbert Blumer and the Chicago tradition* by M. Hammersley. *Contemporary Sociology, 20,* 160-161.

Csikszentmihalyi, M. (1975). *Beyond boredom and anxiety: The experience of play in work and games.* San Francisco: Jossey-Bass.

Denzin, N. K., & Lincoln, Y. S. (1994). Introduction: Entering the field of qualitative research. In N. K. Denzin & Y. S. Lincoln (Eds.), *Handbook of qualitative research* (pp. 1-18). Thousand Oaks, CA: Sage.

Dohan, D., & Sánchez-Jankowski, M. (1998). Using computers to analyze ethnographic field data. In J. Hagen & K. S. Cook (Eds.), *Annual review of sociology* (Vol. 24, pp. 477-498). Palo Alto, CA: Annual Reviews.

Dubin, R. (1992). *Central life interests: Creative individualism in a complex world.* New Brunswick, NJ: Transaction.

Fine, G. A. (1998). *Morel tales: The culture of mushrooming.* Cambridge, MA: Harvard University Press.

Glaser, B. G. (1978). *Theoretical sensitivity: Advances in the methodology of grounded theory.* Mill Valley, CA: Sociology Press.

Glaser, B. G. (1995). *Grounded theory 1984–1994* (Vol. 1). Mill Valley, CA: Sociology Press.

Glaser, B. G., & Strauss, A. L. (1967). *The discovery of grounded theory: Strategies for qualitative research.* Beverly Hills, CA: Sage.

Goffman, E. (1967). *Interaction ritual: Essays in face-to-face behavior.* Chicago: Aldine.

Goffman, E. (1974). *Frame analysis: An essay on the organization of experience.* New York: Harper & Row.

Hagstrom, W. O. (1966). What is the meaning of Santa Claus? *American Sociologist, 1,* 248-252.

Harrison, A. (1998). *Consumers' view of coordination, their transition experiences, and health system performance.* Unpublished doctoral dissertation, University of Calgary.

Harrison, A., Pablo, A., & Verhoef, M. (1999). The consumer's role in co-ordination: Making sense of transitions in health care. In A. Mark & S. Dopson (Eds.), *Organisational behaviour in health care: The research agenda* (pp. 47-62). London: Macmillan.

Hathaway, A. D. (1995). *Marijuana and lifestyle: Exploring tolerable deviance.* Unpublished master's thesis, University of Calgary.

Hathaway, A. D. (1997a). Marijuana and lifestyle: Exploring tolerable deviance. *Deviant Behavior, 18,* 213-233.

Hathaway, A. D. (1997b). Marijuana and tolerance: Revisiting Becker's sources of control. *Deviant Behavior, 18,* 103-125.

Hunter, A. C., & Manley, M. C. (1986). On the task content of work. *Canadian Review of Sociology and Anthropology, 23,* 47-71.

Kaplan, A. (1964). *The conduct of inquiry: Methodology for behavioral science.* San Francisco: Chandler.

Katz, J. (1983). A theory of qualitative methodology: The social system of analytic fieldwork. In R. M. Emerson (Ed.), *Contemporary field research: A collection of readings* (pp. 127-148). Prospect Heights, IL: Waveland.

Kirk, J., & Miller, M. L. (1986). *Reliability and validity in qualitative research* (Sage University Papers Series on Qualitative Research Methods, Vol. 1). Beverly Hills, CA: Sage.

Lacey, A. R. (1986). *A dictionary of philosophy* (2nd ed.). London: Routledge & Kegan Paul.

Lieblich, A., Tuval-Mashiach, R., & Zilber, T. (1998). *Narrative research: Readings, analysis, and interpretation* (Sage University Papers Series on Applied Social Research Methods, Vol. 47). Thousand Oaks, CA: Sage.

Lofland, J. A. (1976). *Doing social life: The qualitative study of human interaction in natural settings.* New York: John Wiley.

Lofland, J. A. (1995). Analytic ethnography: Features, failings, and futures. *Journal of Contemporary Ethnography, 24,* 30-67.

Lofland, J. A., & Lofland, L. H. (1995). *Analyzing social settings: A guide to qualitative observation and analysis* (3rd ed.). Belmont, CA: Wadsworth.

McCall, G. J., & Simmons, J. L. (Eds.). (1969). *Issues in participant observation: A text and reader.* Reading, MA: Addison-Wesley.

Mead, M. (1972). *Blackberry winter: My earliest years.* New York: William Morrow.

Merton, R. K. (1957). *Social theory and social structure* (rev. ed.). Glencoe, IL: Free Press.

Mills, C. W. (1959). *The sociological imagination.* New York: Grove.

Morse, J. M. (1994). Designing funded qualitative research. In N. K. Denzin & Y. S. Lincoln (Eds.), *Handbook of qualitative research* (pp. 220-235). Thousand Oaks, CA: Sage.

Palys, T. (1997). *Research decisions: Quantitative and qualitative perspectives* (2nd ed.). Toronto, ON: Harcourt Brace Canada.

Perry, B. G. (Frankel). (2000). Beginning anew: Doing qualitative research. *Canadian Journal of Sociology, 25,* 97-107.

64

Prus, R. (1987). Generic social processes: Maximizing conceptual development in ethnographic research. *Journal of Contemporary Ethnography, 16,* 250-293.

Reinharz, S. (1979). *On becoming a social scientist.* San Francisco, CA: Jossey-Bass.

Riessman, C. K. (1993). *Narrative analysis* (Sage University Papers Series on Qualitative Research Methods, Vol. 30). Newbury Park, CA: Sage.

Rose, D. (1990). *Living the ethnographic life* (Sage University Papers Series on Qualitative Research Methods, Vol. 23). Newbury Park, CA: Sage.

Sethi, S. (1994). *The dialectic in becoming a mother: Experiencing the postpartum phenomenon.* Unpublished doctoral dissertation, University of Colorado.

Sethi, S. (1995). The dialectic in becoming a mother: Experiencing a postpartum phenomenon. *Scandinavian Journal of Caring Sciences, 9,* 235-244.

Shaffir, W. B., & Stebbins, R. A. (1991). *Experiencing fieldwork: An inside view of qualitative research in the social sciences.* Newbury Park, CA: Sage.

Smith, N. J. (1996). Young women's narratives regarding the development of their occupational aspirations: An initial analysis. In J. Knuf (Ed.), *Proceedings of Fourth International Conference on Narrative* (pp. 301-308). Lexington: University of Kentucky, College of Communications and Information Studies.

Smith, N. J. (1997). *Understanding the development of occupational aspirations in young women: A qualitative analysis.* Unpublished doctoral dissertation, University of Calgary.

Smith, N. J. (in press). Development of young women's aspirations: A qualitative study with implications for education. *Gender and Education.*

Sorensen, J. (1998). *Inmate experiences in wildlife rehabilitation.* Unpublished master's thesis, University of Calgary.

Stebbins, R. A. (1975). *Teachers and meaning: Definitions of classroom situations.* Leiden, The Netherlands: E. J. Brill.

Stebbins, R. A. (1978, November). Toward amateur sociology: A proposal for the profession. *American Sociologist, 13,* 239-247.

Stebbins, R. A. (1979). *Amateurs: On the margin between work and leisure.* Beverly Hills, CA: Sage.

Stebbins, R. A. (1981). Science amators? Rewards and costs in amateur astronomy and archaeology. *Journal of Leisure Research, 13,* 289-304.

Stebbins, R. A. (1990). *The laugh-makers: Stand-up comedy as art, business, and lifestyle.* Montreal, QC and Kingston, ON: McGill-Queen's University Press.

Stebbins, R. A. (1992a). *Amateurs, professionals, and serious leisure.* Montreal, QC and Kingston, ON: McGill-Queen's University Press.

Stebbins, R. A. (1992b). Concatenated exploration: Notes on a neglected type of longitudinal research. *Quality and Quantity, 26,* 435-442.

Stebbins, R. A. (1993a). *Canadian football: The view from the helmet.* Toronto, ON: Canadian Scholars Press.

Stebbins, R. A. (1993b). *Career, culture, and social psychology in a variety art: The magician.* Malabar, FL: Krieger.

Stebbins, R. A. (1996). *The barbershop singer: Inside the social world of a musical hobby.* Toronto, ON: University of Toronto Press.

Stebbins, R. A. (1997a). Casual leisure: A conceptual statement. *Leisure Studies, 16,* 17-25.

Stebbins, R. A. (1997b). Exploratory research as an antidote to theoretical stagnation in leisure studies. *Loisir et Société/Society and Leisure, 20,* 421-434.

Stebbins, R. A. (1997c). Meaning, fragmentation, and exploration: Bêtes noires of leisure science. *Leisure Sciences, 19,* 281-284.

Stewart, A. (1998). *The ethnographer's method.* Thousand Oaks, CA: Sage.

Urdang Associates. (1985). *A dictionary of philosophy* (2nd rev. ed.). London: Macmillan.

Van den Hoonaard, W. C. (1997). *Working with sensitizing concepts: Analytical field research* (Sage University Papers Series on Qualitative Research Methods, Vol. 41). Thousand Oaks, CA: Sage.

Van Maanen, J. (1988). *Tales from the field: On writing ethnography.* Chicago: University of Chicago Press.

Van Maanen, J. (1998). Different strokes: Qualitative research in the *Administrative Science Quarterly* from 1956 to 1996. In J. Van Maanen (Ed.), *Qualitative studies in organizations* (pp. ix-xxxii). Thousand Oaks, CA: Sage.

Vogt, W. P. (1999). *Dictionary of statistics & methodology: A nontechnical guide for the social sciences* (2nd ed.). Thousand Oaks, CA: Sage.

Volkart, E. H. (1951). *Social behavior and personality: Contributions of W. I. Thomas to theory and social research.* New York: Social Science Research Council.

Webb, E. J., Campbell, D. T., Schwartz, R. D., Sechrest, L., & Grove, J. B. (1981). *Nonreactive measures in the social sciences* (2nd ed.). Boston, MA: Houghton Mifflin.

Wolcott, H. F. (1990). *Writing up qualitative research* (Sage University Papers Series on Qualitative Research Methods, Vol. 20). Newbury Park, CA: Sage.

ABOUT THE AUTHOR

Robert A. Stebbins, FRSC, received his PhD in 1964 from the University of Minnesota. He is Professor in, and former Head of, the Department of Sociology at the University of Calgary. He has also taught at Memorial University of Newfoundland and the University of Texas at Arlington. He served as president of the Social Science Federation of Canada in 1991 and 1992, after having served as president of the Canadian Sociology and Anthropology Association in 1988 and 1989. His research interests include humor, work, leisure, the work and leisure dimensions of deviance, and the leisure basis of francophone communities outside Quebec. He has published more than 115 journal articles and book chapters as well as 23 books. In the past two decades, his work has centered primarily on *serious leisure* (a term he coined in 1982), as expressed in exploratory research dating from 1973 on amateurs (actors, magicians, musicians, archaeologists, astronomers, baseball and football players, and stand-up comics); hobbyists (barbershop singers, cultural tourists); and career volunteers (urban francophones). He recently completed an adult education guide to serious leisure titled *After Work: The Search for an Optimal Leisure Lifestyle* and an analysis of French Canada, *The French Enigma: Survival and Development in Canada's Francophone Societies. New Directions in the Theory and Research of Serious Leisure* will be published in 2001. He is presently gathering exploratory data on low- and high-risk kayakers, mountain climbers, and snowboarders in the Canadian Rockies. In 1996, Stebbins was elected Fellow of the Academy of Leisure Sciences and, in 1999, Fellow of the Royal Society of Canada.

Qualitative Research Methods

Series Editor
JOHN VAN MAANEN
Massachusetts Institute of Technology

Associate Editors:
Peter K. Manning, *Michigan State University*
& Marc L. Miller, *University of Washington*

Other volumes in this series listed on outside back cover